Let's Dive
Begin the Adventure

The Sub Aqua Association
Club Diver Manual

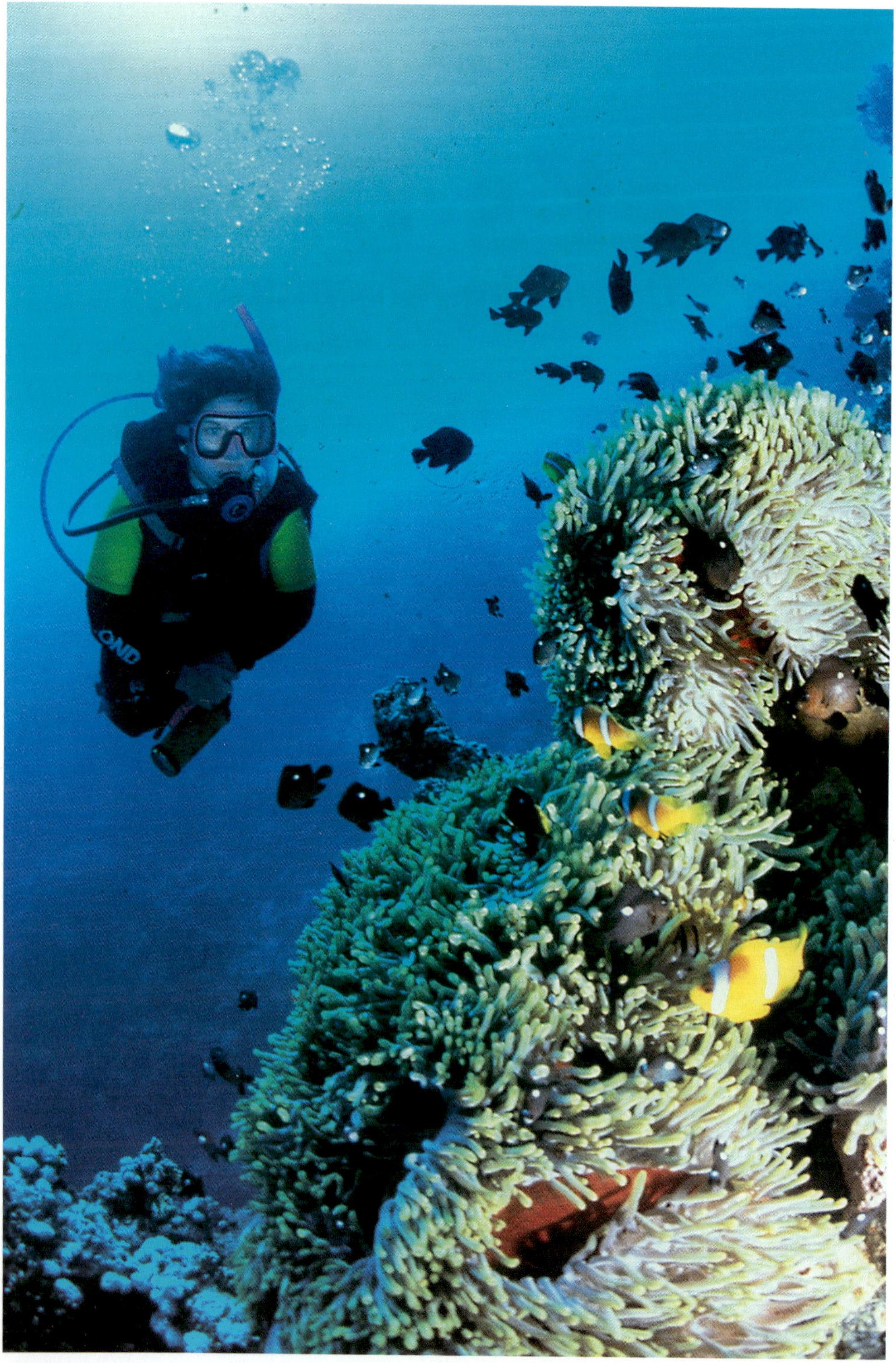

Let's Dive
Begin the Adventure

Colin Brittain

The Sub Aqua Association
Club Diver Manual

VICTORY PUBLISHING

Disclaimer

Recreational diving is a potentially hazardous sport and if safe diving practices are not adhered to it can expose a person to substantial risks, which may lead to serious injury in extreme circumstances. Sub aqua diving is a sport that requires specialised training, equipment and experience. It is not an activity that can be mastered by simply reading a book or watching a video. Training given by a fully qualified instructor is the only way to prepare the diver for safe open water diving.

This book is not intended to be a substitute for the above and is designed to supplement training given by an instructor. The aim of the book is intended to be a source of reference.

The author, publisher, and manufacturers represented within this book are not liable for any damage, injury or death, which may result from scuba diving activities, with respect to any information contained in the book.

SUB AQUA ASSOCIATION
26 Breckfield Road North
Liverpool
L5 4NH

Telephone: 0151 287 1001   Fax: 0151 287 1026
E-mail contact: admin@saa.org.uk
www.saa.org.uk

First Edition 2001
ISBN 0-9541341-0-9
© Copyright 2001 Sub Aqua Association

All rights reserved. No part of this publication may be reproduced or transmitted in any form or by any means, electronic or mechanical, including photocopying, recording, or any information storage and retrieval system, without permission in writing from the publishers.

Published by:
Victory Publishing
Hill Park House, 65 Hill Park Crescent, Plymouth PL4 8JW
Tel: 01752 294070   Fax: 01752 291337   Email: victory@tinyworld.co.uk

Designed and produced by:
Enigma Creative
68 Trevillis Park, Liskeard, Cornwall PL14 4EQ
Tel: 07812 797811   Email: mail@enigmacreative.com
www.enigmacreative.com

CONTENTS

Acknowledgements 6
Foreword 7
Author's Introduction 8
The Attractions of Sub Aqua diving 9
The History of Scuba Diving 14

CHAPTER 1	The Sub Aqua Association	16
CHAPTER 2	Introduction to Basic Equipment	20
CHAPTER 3	Protective Clothing, Scuba Equipment and Equipment Maintenance	28
CHAPTER 4	Practical Diver Training	44
CHAPTER 5	Pressure, Physics and the Diver	55
CHAPTER 6	Respiration, Circulation and Air Endurance	62
CHAPTER 7	Diving Disorders and Decompression Illness	67
CHAPTER 8	Accident Avoidance and Rescue Procedures	76
CHAPTER 9	Diving Air and Deep Diving	86
CHAPTER 10	SAA Bühlmann Tables, Dive Computers and Avoiding Decompression Illness	95
CHAPTER 11	Open Water Diving, Dive Planning and Underwater Navigation	99
CHAPTER 12	Diving for Pleasure	105

APPENDIXES 123
GLOSSARY 129
INDEX 138
BIBLIOGRAPHY 144

Acknowledgements

The first edition of the Sub Aqua Association Club Diver Manual is the end product of many contributors all of whom are specialists in their own field

The Sub Aqua Association greatly acknowledges the efforts of the following persons who helped in the production of this manual:

Stuart Bryan
Roy Bunn
Bryony Chapman
Danny Connolly
Dave Dresser
Paul Johnson-Ross
Neil Kenley
North East Underwater Centre (Denney Diving)
John Parry
Steve Reid and Colleagues of Cloud Nine Divers
Courtney Sharp
Dawn Simpson

Line Drawing Acknowledgements

Our gratitude goes to the following people for accepting the challenge of contributing with line drawings to the manual:

Frank Foster	47, 50, 63, 64, 65, 66, 68, 69, 70, 71, 72, 73
Albert Güillen	12, 37, 62, 67, 91, 92
Sarah Turner	10, 15, 51, 52, 76, 77, 78, 79, 80, 108

Photographic Acknowledgements

We would like to thank the following people for allowing the use of copyrighted illustrations required to produce the manual:

Colin Brittain	7, 31, 97, 111, 113
Buddy / AP Valves	38, 60, 84, 85
Neil Cunningham	109, 110
Cindy Gradin for the image taken by her brother the late Wes Gradin	99
Mark Hutchinson	20, 21, 40, 88, 103
Colin Martin	106, 107
John Parry	86, 116
Gavin Parsons	3, 82, 94, 98, 104, 114, 115
	Diver over tropical reef, rear cover
Sea & Sea (IST)	13, 14, 16, 17, 19, 39, 41, 43, 44, 89, 90
David Stephens	2, 23, 46, 48, 49, 53, 54, 55, 56, 58, 59, 61, 74, 93, 100,
	Lionfish in Cornwall, rear cover
Dawn Simpson	1, 112
Underwater Kinetics / Dive Rite	27, 33, 34, 35, 36, 45, 83
Simon Volpe	9, 105
Alan Wastell	5, 6, 11, 18, 22, 24, 25, 26, 28, 29, 30, 32, 42, 75, 87, 96
Cy Willis	8, 81
Ian Wright	4, 95, 101, 102
	Underwater photographer under a boat, rear cover

Foreword

Diving is fun, adventure and pleasure underwater. It is a modern leisure time sport for women and men – it can be enjoyed by everyone, old or young. The pioneers of the modern diving sport, Hans Hass and Jacques-Yves Cousteau, started to explore the underwater world more than 60 years ago and are the fathers of diving.

Cousteau founded in 1959 with 15 representatives of different nations the CMAS (Confédération Mondiale des Activités Subaquatiques) – the World Underwater Federation – the only organisation representing all underwater activities. Today the CMAS has more than 100 member countries. The Sub Aqua Association joined the family and became a member of this World Underwater Federation in 1996.

Diving is becoming more and more popular. You will need to seek an understanding of a different world – this book will help you in this regard and enable you to dive safely. You do not need to be a champion swimmer to take up the sport, but you need competent and qualified training. Experience should be built up gradually, don't rush or be pushed into diving when or where you don't feel confident. This book will be your guide into a new, fascinating world.

You will have a great time – remember that the best diver is not the one who goes deepest, but the one who comes back every time.

More and more people are diving and enjoying it. You do not know what you are missing until you have tried it. (You give it a try.)

Good Luck

Walter Tichy
President Technical Committee CMAS
Vice-President CMAS
Vienna

Author's Introduction

Throughout Britain we were amazed to see Martha Holmes using the revolutionary "Bubble" helmet. Who could forget Anneka Rice and Ulrika Jonsson? Well-known television personalities such as David Jason (*Only Fools and Horses*), James Crossley, better known as "Hunter" from the television show *Gladiators* programme, and Mark Wingett, otherwise known as "Carver" from the hit television series *The Bill,* all have one thing in common – their love of "sub aqua diving", even though punishing schedules mean underwater time is often limited.

Welcome to the exciting sport of sub aqua diving. Three-quarters of the world is underwater. Diving takes the individual into a new dimension where many beautiful and awesome dive sites await the intrepid diver. The underwater world can be so enchanting. Diving is a sport which takes the individual into an 'alien' environment. Proper training is essential to enjoying the sport. Safe diving is only done once the student has completed a certified diver-training course with a certified diver-training agency such as the Sub Aqua Association (SAA). Diving is a sport that cannot be learnt safely by simply watching a video or reading a book.

Before embarking to open water the trainee will be taught both theoretically and practically what sub aqua diving is all about. Recreational diver training is both fun and easy, but there are skills that must be satisfactorily completed if the individual is to get the best out of the sport. It is only after completing a certification course that the newly qualified diver is able to understand the dangers associated with recreational scuba diving. Knowledge of diving equipment and theory is essential to enhancing the diver's enjoyment of the sport.

This manual contains a wealth of material for the new student. This is just the start of a wonderful journey. Learning to dive is a unique experience in its own right. This manual has been developed to be used alongside a certification course given by a qualified SAA Instructor.

The information presented here will show the reader the essentials for safe and enjoyable diving. Throughout the manual each topic is presented with illustrations so that the reader can clearly understand what is involved.

Any information contained within the manual relates to diving and not to any specific person and must not be construed as such. Any practical diving or theoretical issues should be discussed directly with your instructor.

Colin Brittain
Sub Aqua Diving Instructor

The Attractions Of Sub Aqua Diving

Sub aqua diving is one of the fastest growing sports and is often featured on television. There is no substitute for "real" diving, in an environment where almost the only sound you will hear is that of your exhaled breath. Images of tropical waters allow the would-be diver to experience the thrill provided by the adventure and challenge of sub aqua diving. Maritime history, marine life in its natural habitat, underwater photography, archaeology and the chance to possibly find something unique are available prospects for the avid diver.

Figure 1 A wall dive in the Red Sea

The temperate waters of the UK provide many opportunities for underwater photography including a variety of marine life and natural features. As well as providing a haven for wildlife, wrecks allow the diver the chance to explore aspects of maritime history. Wrecks from two world wars litter the seabed around the coast of Britain. Many wrecks are war graves and should be treated with the respect and regulations that cover this.

Experience for the first time underwater changes in colour, listen as sounds become amplified as you submerge below the waves for the first time, share with your buddy the adrenaline rush. Back on the surface you can share your experiences with friends and relatives. Many clubs organise regular dive excursions and many organise and undertake extended dive expeditions or holidays to tropical destinations. With so many dive centres situated throughout the world it is now often possible to combine a trip away with a diving holiday.

Figure 2 Rebreather diver with a friendly seal

Figure 3 Diver exploring a wreck in Tenerife

Figure 4 Jewel Anemone commonly found in Cornish waters

Diving in safety

Learning to scuba dive in the UK gives the diver a good foundation for dives in warmer waters. Diving equipment has progressed to a high standard allowing safer and more comfortable dives.

It is possible to enter a diving shop and purchase all the equipment required for scuba diving without any certification and then go straight into the sea. Without proper training the diver would be ill prepared to deal with difficulties which could present themselves. Recreational diving is a sport that can only be learnt by completing a recognised certification course, with assistance from a fully qualified instructor.

Practical training ensures the diver is fully aware of what may be encountered. It is not safe or prudent for someone to attempt to learn to dive by merely watching a video or reading a book.

Learning to dive

Learning to dive should not be thought of as a complex task, but merely a means to prepare the student for safe practical open water diving. The training has two objectives:

- To ensure the diver has the knowledge and skills to dive safely and enjoyably.
- To ensure the diver has an understanding of the risks involved in diving, and the ability to deal effectively with any problems.

Learning to dive is broken into three separate modules.

Theory lessons

The student is presented with theory lessons designed to teach the knowledge required. The range of subjects covered include selecting scuba equipment, basic physics and physiology,

Figure 5 Classroom lesson

diving disorders, along with a look at diving accident avoidance and decompression tables.

Confined/sheltered practical sessions

The student will be introduced to important practical skills needed by every diver. The skills are taught in the safe confines of sheltered water, in most cases a warm swimming pool. Practical sheltered water lessons are broken down into easy stages, with repetition, to ensure foundation skills are mastered to the satisfaction of your instructor.

Open water dives

Once the instructor is satisfied that the diver is competent with his skills he is introduced to real diving in a confined body of water. This can be anything from a flooded inland quarry to the ocean when conditions allow. This is the chance to put into practice all the things learnt in the pool. At last the student gets his first real taste of recreational sport diving.

When learning to dive your instructor will make natural progression simple. Theory lessons and practical skills develop at a pace to suit the student. Theory knowledge and practical skills required for safe open water diving are broken down into easy stages and presented in an understandable progressive structure.

The course will culminate in practical skills assessments, and a multiple choice knowledge review to ensure the topics presented in theory lessons have been understood and absorbed.

Figure 6 Pool training lesson

Figure 7 Students embarking on their first sea dive

The History of Scuba Diving

It is reported that rudimentary diving bells have existed since early 300 BC. In 1690 Edmund Halley patented the first bell with a pressurised air supply that was supplied from the surface. The bell, which was open at the bottom, was large enough for two divers.

Halley's bell inspired other inventors to have a go at their own version of the diving bell and an Englishman, John Lethbridge, designed and built a long oak barrel which he could use to salvage treasure. Pulling himself along the seabed he would dive for up to half an hour. When he

Figure 8 Example of equipment used prior to SCUBA equipment

became low on air he was hauled to the surface where fresh air was pumped into the barrel using bellows, before dropping back to the seabed.

Things were pretty quiet for around a hundred years until two English brothers, Charles and John Deane, designed a diving suit and helmet that utilised air from the surface. One of the drawbacks to the system was that the helmet did not seal to the suit so if the diver bent over too far the helmet would flood. This was, however, a general success and went on to become the standard equipment for nearly 150 years.

The biggest improvement to the 'Deanes' design came in 1836, when German inventor Augustus Siebe designed a system with the helmet sealed to a watertight rubber dry suit. This was essentially the prototype for many of the hard hat systems in use today.

In 1865 a steel cylinder that could be filled with compressed air and worn on the diver's back was introduced. Patented as the 'Aerophore' the unit was designed to deliver air on demand (demand valve). The air was fed to the diver via a valve attached to a breathing tube and mouthpiece. Initially air was pumped into the cylinder from the surface, although the diver had the facility to disconnect for a few moments.

Captain Yves Le Prier further modified the unit in 1933 combining the demand valve with a high-pressure cylinder. This gave the diver freedom from the then restrictive surface supply hoses.

It was not until 1942-43 that the equipment as we know it started to be developed. Captain Jacques-Yves Cousteau and Emile Gagnan worked together with a car regulator, which when finished was the first truly effective 'demand valve'. This was the beginning of S.C.U.B.A. (self-contained underwater breathing apparatus) commonly used today.

In 1993 the 50th anniversary of scuba diving was celebrated around the world. Scuba diving finally came of age. Sport diving is a growing sport enjoyed by people of all ages.

In the last ten years many sports divers have turned to a range of gases to alter dive profiles, giving added safety factors. With the use of mixed breathing gases many divers carry out dives in excess of the 50 metre recommended limit for air. This type of diving, which is referred to as 'Technical' continues to push back the boundaries.

Figure 9 Modern day diver

Chapter 1 The Sub Aqua Association

The Sub Aqua Association (SAA) was formed in 1976. Originally formed as a register of non-affiliated clubs, as the number of clubs grew there was soon a call for a more formal organisation, one with a central representative body. The SAA has continued its success rate and new clubs are formed each year.

An important feature of all clubs is their independence. Whilst the SAA will not interfere with the normal day-to-day running of any club, they are only a telephone call away for assistance. The SAA Training Programme has been developed to ensure that the beginner moves through the grades in an enjoyable and progressive way. Each new level of training builds comfortably on what has previously been learnt, both in the classroom and in the pool. The student will be invited into open water when the instructor thinks it is appropriate. This will be in a controlled safe environment.

The SAA is an internationally recognised diver-training organisation, principally based in the UK. There are, however, clubs in other parts of the world.

Summary of diving qualifications

Elementary Diver
An elementary diver is fully pool trained, but inexperienced in open water. When diving in open water a suitably qualified diver of dive leader grade or above must accompany an elementary diver.

Open Water Diver
An open water diver has additional practical training experience. The diver must be accompanied by a dive leader or above.

Club Diver
A club diver is a qualified open water diver who, having gained more experience and additional skills may dive with other club divers or above. However, a club diver is not considered to have enough experience to take an elementary diver or open water divers on open water dives.

Dive Leader
The dive leader is a diver who has additional practical experience and higher theory ability. The dive leader may lead other divers on open water dives. The dive leader may dive with divers of any grade.

Dive Supervisor
A dive supervisor is an experienced and responsible diver, with a proven ability to organise and lead club expeditions.

Dive Master
The dive master has received the grade through nationally conducted examinations. The dive master has proved to have attained a higher than average level of knowledge and ability. The dive master is able to organise divers to achieve major tasks and underwater projects.

The SAA welcomes divers from all training organisations. Training is available to assist divers from other training organisations to cross over to the equivalent SAA diver grade. The training is simple and introduces the Sub Aqua Association method of diver training. The following table represents the major diver training organisation equivalent grades:

Administration
Administration of the SAA is by the National Council, which is elected from SAA members. Executive officers are unpaid volunteers giving their time freely to represent the membership. Officers of the executive are made up of:

Chairman
The Chairman is responsible for promoting the SAA with other sports councils and interested parties.

Vice Chairman
The role of the vice-chairman is to deputise for the chairman in his absence.

Secretary
It is the secretary who is responsible for club enquiries, arranging meetings, sorting club membership details and general members' details.

Treasurer
All SAA financial concerns including subscription and insurance matters are dealt with by the treasurer.

National Diving Officer (NDO)
All diving, training and safety matters within the organisation fall within the responsibility of the NDO. These include training manuals and registration of all instructor courses. The NDO liaises closely with the chairman on diving matters with other interested parties. The National Diving Officer is responsible for appointing persons such as:

- Decompression Officer
- Medical Advisor

Executive Member
The executive member is the members representative on the Executive and is responsible for communications with the membership. The Executive member is also responsible for awards and presentations, such as the AGM within the Association.

Regional Representatives represent the UK regions and deal with the members and club queries. With the help of the NDO they co-ordinate courses and national examinations throughout the regions.

The executive meets 6 times a year and the Regional Representatives meet with the executive as the National Council twice each year. The Annual General Meeting is a major event, which is open to all members.

Affiliations
The SAA is the only diver training organisation in Britain that is affiliated to the World Underwater Federation – Confédération Mondiale Des Activités Subaquatiques (CMAS) and authorised to issue CMAS certification in the UK.

The SAA is affiliated to the International Association of Nitrox and Technical Divers (IANTD) and Technical Divers International (TDI), which are two of the largest 'technical divers' training organisations.

The SAA devised its own Nitrox courses for members, which have dual status. The qualifying diver will receive either an SAA/TDI or SAA/IANTD C-Card (qualification card) according to the status of the instructor running the course. If the student wishes to pursue Nitrox courses outside of the SAA they will already have the base qualification from which to start, ensuring they do not have start from scratch.

The SAA was the first recreational diver-training agency to be approved to provide rebreather training, and is an approved Draeger Training Agency, receiving formal accreditation for their own courses when using the Draeger unit.

The SAA works closely with a number of other organisations involved in diving, such as the Marine Conservation Society, and the Nautical Archaeological Society, and encourages members to participate in their projects to provide an extra purpose to diving.

Insurance
Insurance cover automatically covers individuals joining the SAA once their application has been processed. The cover primarily consists of 'Third Party' cover and 'Personal Accident' cover, which is unique to the association.

How do you join a club?
The first step is to ring head office to identify your local club and enquire when they meet. Many clubs have meetings at swimming pools where training is being given. Swimming pools are often good places to find out about the local diving club. At seaside resorts you can find out

from divers you talk to where the club meets.

The second step is to go along to a meeting session and introduce yourself. Sometimes clubs hold an annual 'open evening'. These evenings are ideal taster sessions where members of the public get the opportunity to 'Try a Dive'. At these sessions you will be introduced to the leading figures in the club. At the end of the session if you feel the sport is for you then you will be invited to become a member of the club. Once you have chosen to participate in this exciting sport and made the moves to become a member of your local club and with a medical completed your training can begin.

Learning to dive may seem a daunting task, with theory lessons and pool sessions to do, however this is not true. The beginner will be taught the skills and knowledge that are required to embark on safe open water diving in a safe controlled environment with qualified instructors. Entry-level courses are designed to make learning to dive fun and easy. Your instructor will repeat any skills you are not happy with until they have been mastered.

Who can join a club?
Membership of the SAA is open to anyone medically fit. Junior divers who are medically fit are entitled to begin training at twelve years of age at the discretion of each club. Diving is enjoyed by men and women of all ages, from 12 upwards – all that is required is good medical health and a good level of fitness. A few medical conditions may preclude a person from diving, such as any serious respiratory or circulatory disorder, heart disease or serious head injuries. Most people are able to meet the demands of sub aqua diving. If, however, you have any doubts, then you are advised to seek advice from a doctor familiar with diving medical conditions. The SAA is also pleased to offer advice for people with physical disabilities who wish to embark on recreational diving. When you join the SAA you will be required to have some basic swimming ability. Olympic standard is not required as divers 'fin' rather than 'swim'. In the fitness test the trainee is expected to swim, 200 metres freestyle, and recover 3 objects from the bottom of a swimming pool (1.5 metres maximum depth).

What happens when you join a club?
Once your membership is processed you will be issued with a student pack. Inside this you will find;
- Your qualification logbook. Inside this all your theory lessons and pool sessions are marked up. The qualification is awarded once all the requirements have been met for each individual grade.
- A copy of the Sub Aqua Association Constitution.

Each month your club receives a copy of the **Scuba World** magazine, which is the magazine affiliated to the organisation. As a member of the SAA you are entitled to discount on the subscription fee to the magazine. You are also eligible for further discount on goods from the Association mailshop, run from the headquarters. Full members of the SAA are entitled to attend additional training courses when they meet the pre-requisite grades.

The membership fee, which is valid for one year, is made up of two parts. The first part is sent to the headquarters, whilst the remainder is kept within your club to help maintain club facilities such as compressors, boats and diving equipment. Full diving members retain full voting rights whilst their membership is valid.

Being a member
Those clubs with sufficient equipment will be able to loan it to students until they obtain their own, normally within the first year. Additional courses are run through the region to expand the theory and practical elements of diver training. Members are welcome to attend conferences and the Annual General Meeting (AGM) held nationally. Many of the larger clubs

have their own clubhouse used for regular meetings and social activities. Clubs provide a wealth of experience, to which the student has access. Club meetings provide the ideal environment for divers to share their experiences and knowledge.

Your role in a club

As you progress within a club you should be willing to put something back in to developing it. The student should be keen to get involved. The student who offers assistance will be rapidly accepted and welcomed.

Students are advised to follow rules that have been set by their club. Although in practical terms there are few rules (recommendations are better than rules) they are there to protect you the student and other divers. They are not there to impede anybody's actions but to help everyone enjoy themselves in safety. Each individual club will have its own rules regarding club diving and training procedures. Many centre on simple common sense.

The student is encouraged to attend lectures on time, equipped with the items advised by the instructor. Reading up on the proposed lecture will aid understanding of the lecture. The student should try to attend each lecture. Some clubs may find re-arranging additional lectures difficult. Any missed lessons (practical or theory) will slow the student's progress down.

Chapter 2 Introduction To Basic Equipment

The first pieces of equipment normally purchased by the student are likely to be mask, fins and snorkel, otherwise known as "basic equipment". Careful consideration should be given when selecting the right type of equipment, as some equipment is not designed for sub aqua diving and may not be appropriate for the demands to be placed on it whilst diving. There are essential features to look out for when buying equipment. Your instructor will explain what to look for during your theory lessons.

There are a variety of ways to obtain diving equipment, including mail-order catalogues, sporting goods shops and stores that specialise in dive equipment. The best choice for all your equipment needs is a local dive shop. There are a number of justifications for this;

- There is no substitute for being at the shop in person allowing you to actually see and try the equipment first hand.
- When purchasing suits the proprietor is likely to have experience in measuring you properly.
- Some larger shops may have access to a pool enabling actual use of the equipment.
- Your local shop assistant can offer a valuable source of specialist advice.
- Your local shop can offer full service arrangements.
- Ask your instructor or an experienced diver to accompany you.

Mask

Our eyes are designed to function in an air environment and it is the function of the mask to provide a layer of air between the eyes and water. Underwater everything would just appear unfocused without a mask.

One of the most important features when choosing a mask is to make sure that it is fitted with tempered glass. The cheaper types of mask are generally fitted with plastic that can easily shatter. A mask with tempered glass is designed to withstand the effects of increased water pressure. A mask that is fitted with tempered glass will be marked with the letter "T" etched onto the front of the glass. The nose must be enclosed so that the artificial air space within the mask can be equalised as the diver descends, this also allows the nose to be pinched to equalise the pressure on the ears. Goggles do not enclose the nose and it is not possible to equalise the pressure within the mask, for this reason goggles are not acceptable for scuba diving.

When choosing a mask it is important to make sure that it fits correctly and doesn't leak. A mask that constantly leaks is at best irritating and a discomfort, but at worst it can become a hazard and may lead to more serious problems. Most dive shops will give advice to help you choose the right mask to suit you. All masks must have a comfortable skirt, as a mask with a hard skirt will soon become uncomfortable and irritate the diver. A mask which is too tight will leak just as much as a mask that is too loose. Masks are also available with corrective lenses for those who use spectacles.

Masks are classed as either a low volume or high volume mask. This refers to the amount of available air space the mask has between the lens and the eyes. The low volume mask will hold less flooded water, making it easier to clear. The closer the lens is to the eyes, the wider the view is likely to be.

Masks with additional side lenses may increase peripheral vision but also increase the air space volume. Masks with additional lenses also add to the cost of the mask. Some masks are available with purge valves to aid clearing flooded water.

There are two basic types of mask: rubber and silicon. The silicon mask is the more popular of the two types. There are a number of reasons for this:

- It is less likely to irritate the diver with sensitive skin.
- The material is translucent and will therefore allow more light in.

- The mask skirt is generally slightly softer, hence more comfortable.
- Silicon masks last longer than the rubber mask, which tend to perish quicker if left in sunlight.

When choosing a mask it is important to test the fit. A simple way of doing this is to hold it to your face and breathe in through your nose. The mask should stay in place without the use of the strap. If you need to inhale continuously you should choose another mask, one that fits better.

When masks are manufactured the mould is coated in a thin film of lubricant. The lubricant is designed to make it easier to remove the mask. The lubricant must be removed to prevent continual misting. In order to remove the film one of the recommended methods is using a drop of toothpaste or detergent. After washing the lens rinsing the lubricant in fresh water leaves the mask ready for use. This step is only required once, in future use all that is required is for the diver to use a readily available product, saliva, or one of the commercially manufactured products. Without this preparation the mask would fog up all the time.

Fins

Without fins the diver is virtually motionless. Fins provide the diver with a means of propulsion with the minimum of effort. Fins come in two types:

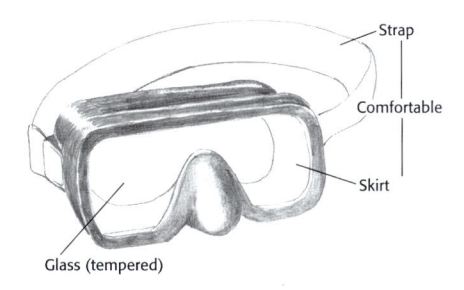

Figure 10 Diving mask attributes

Figure 11 Common diving masks used by divers

Pool/shoe fin

This type of fin is designed for sheltered water such as swimming pools or warm water locations. They come with soft heels and are normally purchased in the same size as your shoe size.

When choosing fins they should be comfortable. If they are a loose fit they may fall off. Care should be taken as manufacturer sizes can differ. A pair of fins that are too hard will be uncomfortable and ineffective and will soon sap the diver's energy and enthusiasm.

Open heel fin

This fin is used primarily by divers in open water. Fins are generally available in small, medium and large sizes. When worn with a semi-dry suit the boot should be tried out wearing a wet suit type boot. The diver should consider the dry suit boot when choosing the size of fins. The fit of the fin should be such that when the chosen boot is worn it would not make the fin uncomfortable.

All fins have common features;
- The fin should be rigid enough to provide the necessary propulsion without being too hard. Open heel fins should include side ribs to strengthen the blade and increase efficiency.
- The fins should have comfortable foot pockets.
- The open heel fin must be equipped with buckles that can be easily adjusted wearing gloves.

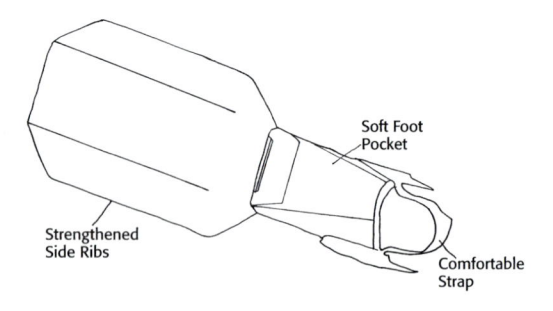

Figure 12 Typical fin attributes

Figure 13 Pool/tropical water fins

Figure 14 Open foot fins

Snorkels

Whilst swimming on the surface without a snorkel the diver would have to constantly lift his head to breathe. This would soon become very tiring. Using a snorkel the diver can observe the underwater world, conserving air in the cylinder.

A snorkel in its simplest form is a 'tube' of around 45cm long with an internal bore of 2-3cm. If the length of the 'tube' is longer the diver will not be able to breathe from it, whilst the short snorkel would constantly flood. If the bore of the tube were restricted then it would inevitably restrict the breathing, if it is excessive the snorkel may flood and the student would find it difficult to clear.

At the lower end of the tube every snorkel should be fitted with a soft mouthpiece. Most snorkels come with mouthpieces that rotate. Careful consideration should be given to purchasing a snorkel. The snorkel may be for occasional use when swimming on the surface in which case a cheaper version will suffice. However, if you intend doing a lot of snorkelling then one of the dearer snorkels might possibly be a better option.

Older snorkels would only have the standard J bend at the bottom. However, most modern snorkels now have a short flexible tube at the bottom, allowing the mouthpiece to hang down out of the way during a dive when it is not being used. Whilst some snorkels come equipped with a device to protect the top, the diver should avoid a snorkel that has any device that closes off the snorkel.

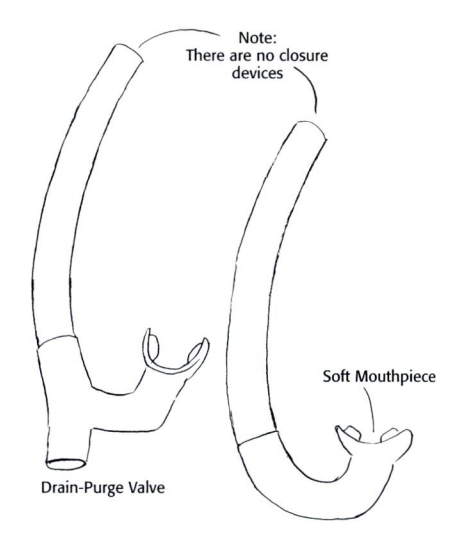

Figure 15 Snorkel characteristics

Figure 16 Basic snorkel

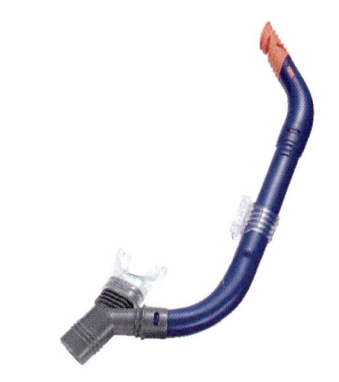

Figure 17 Snorkel with advanced features

Weightbelts

Divers in British climate waters are committed to wearing some form of thermal protection. Unfortunately it is this protection that makes the diver positively buoyant. In order to counteract this buoyancy the diver is forced to wear a weightbelt. The amount of weight required can differ from individual to individual depending on what suit is worn and whether they are diving in fresh water or seawater.

The standard type of weightbelt is a plain 2" webbing belt onto which lead weights are attached until the diver has the correct amount fitted. The lead weights are held in place by weight slides, so that when handing the weightbelt up to a boatman after a dive the weights do not slide off the belt. Depending on the quantity of weight required the diver could choose lead weights in 1kg, 2kg, 3kg or 4kg. Most weights are plastic coated and are available in a variety of colours. With some divers requiring quite an amount of weight manufacturers brought out a simple harness system. This harness fits over the shoulders and encompasses the weightbelt thereby distributing the weight over the body and therefore alleviating the discomfort some belts create on the hips.

Many divers are turning to shot weightbelts for the added comfort they provide. These belts are capable of holding shot weight or pouches of shot enabling the diver to easily add the amount of weight required. Some buoyancy compensators are equipped with pockets that hold shot pouch weights. These eliminate the need for a weightbelt altogether.

When choosing a weightbelt the most important feature is make sure that it has a quick release buckle fitted. The buckle should be of a type that can be released by a diver wearing gloves. Standard buckles allow the diver to adjust the belt as they descend to compensate for suit compression. The buckle can be steel or plastic. Divers are advised to avoid any sort of weightbelt buckle that has some form of locking device. Some divers require weightbelts of around 30lb depending on their circumstances.

Figure 18 Two types of weightbelt

Knives

Contrary to popular belief divers do not wear knives to fight off sharks. The diver's knife is a tool for emergency use. One of the biggest threats to divers underwater is discarded netting/fishing line or ropes. Most divers will carry more than one type of knife, the most common type being the larger knife attached to the diver's leg. This is because of the physical size of the knife. The smaller knife can be attached to the arm or permanently fitted to the buoyancy compensator. If the diver becomes trapped in line, it may be easier to get to the knife attached to the buoyancy compensator. Most divers knives have a pointed blade although they are available with a chisel type edge. The most common type of knife is one which has a straight edge and a serrated edge.

All divers knives are made of stainless steel as normal steel would not withstand the rigours of the saltwater environment. Stainless steel however is not without its drawbacks: whilst lasting longer stainless steel does not hold its edge for long. This means the knife requires regular sharpening. A blunt knife is not much use when you need it in an emergency. Once sharpened the knife should be lightly coated in oil or silicon grease to protect it. The knife should always be kept in its sheath. The knife should also have a small lanyard attached so it cannot be dropped out of its sheath by accident.

Figure 19 Divers knives

Diver bags

The diver must have some means of carrying his equipment. Bags are now available in many colours and types. There seems to be a bag for almost everything, including individual bags for the regulator, the diving suit, for basic equipment (a wet mesh bag) along with bags capable of holding everything in, such as large holdalls to big rucksacks. When choosing a bag the diver should consider the environment for which it is designed. A cheap sports bag will not stand the weight, or wear and tear that diving equipment can produce, along with the saltwater environment in which we frequently dive.

The good dive equipment bag is one that is made from a heavy-duty nylon. Many come coated internally with a plastic coating. This is important if you want to minimise the water seeping out into the boot of your car on the way home. The zip on the bag will last longer if constructed from a plastic material rather than metal which will soon corrode.

Figure 21 A medium sized backpack

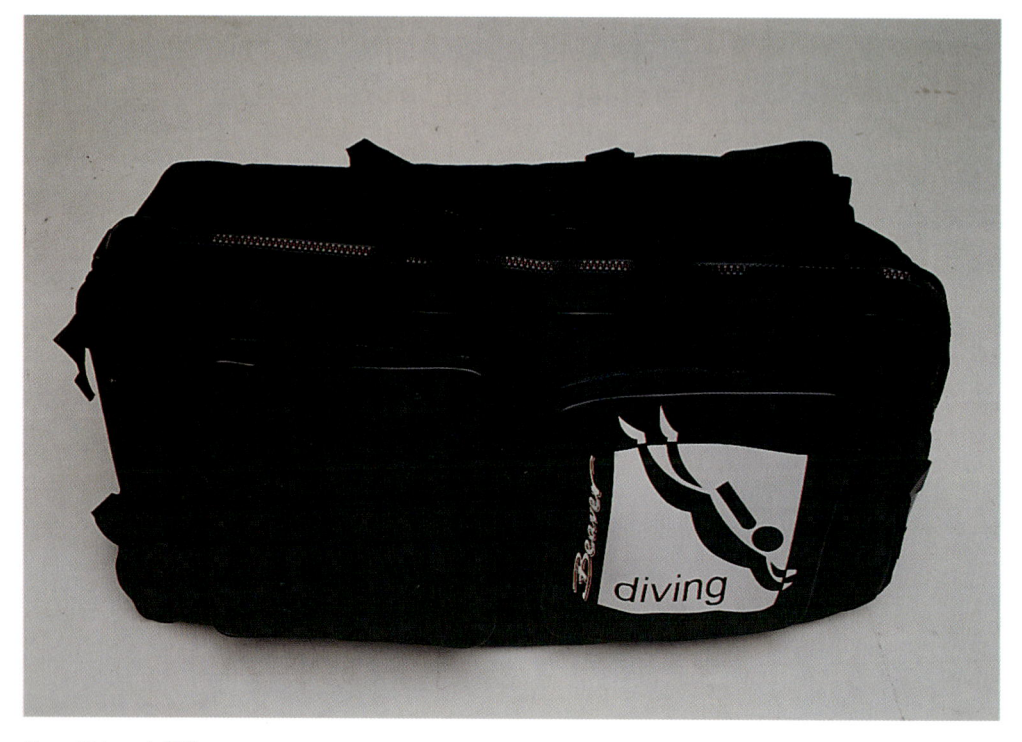

Figure 20 Large holdall

Diver Boxes

Many divers and dive schools are turning to boxes for storing diving equipment instead of the traditional bag. Large plastic boxes are ideally suited to the conditions in which they are used. It is possible to store all your diving equipment in them (minus cylinder and weights). It would soon become apparent to the diver, however, that the divers box would be a problem on a small boat where space is limited.

Figure 22 Diving equipment boxes

Chapter 3 Protective Clothing, Scuba Equipment & Equipment Maintenance

Even in the warmest of water divers require the use of protective clothing. Protective clothing can be used to protect the diver against harmful effects of:
- Cold
- Abrasion
- Pollution
- Hazardous creatures

There are commonly two types of open water diving suit. Both types of suits have their followers and each have qualities unique to the type of suit chosen.

Semi-Drysuits & Wetsuits

These are designed to allow a small amount of water in, forming a thin layer under the suit. In the Semi-drysuit seals at the wrist, ankle and neck or face reduce this quantity of water. It is a commonly held belief that this water acts as an insulator. It is in fact the neoprene foam that the suits are made from that the insulation is derived from. Different thicknesses of suit are available; these include 3mm for tropical waters whilst for the colder waters of the British Isles an 8mm suit is called for. The suit must be a close fit to help prevent cold water 'flushing' through it making the diver cold. However, if the suit is too tight then it may make moving and breathing more difficult.

Drysuits

Drysuits are designed to keep the diver dry. They are intended to be waterproof suits, which have seals at the neck and wrists excluding water entirely. Entry to the suit is made through a strong waterproof zip. Additional insulation may be provided by wearing thermal underclothing, this depends on the drysuit type. Air is a better insulator than water, which has the effect of making drysuits warmer than other suits. As drysuits can be used for buoyancy control, additional training is advised prior to using a drysuit in open water.

The increased cost of a drysuit may be the deciding factor to many divers when choosing a suit. If looked after the drysuit can last many years providing warmth and comfort. The initial investment in the drysuit may be worth the extra cost.

Qualities of diving suits
Semi-Drysuit
- Expanded foam neoprene with neoprene wrist and ankle seals. Often equipped with an integral hood.
- Buoyancy will vary with depth as material becomes compressed or expands.
- Neck and wrist seals help prevent suit 'flushing' (flow of water through suit).

Membrane Drysuit
- Tri-laminate (nylon/rubber) or vulcanised rubber material.
- Neck and wrist seals normally made of latex rubber. Rear shoulder or across-body waterproof zip fitted with integral boots.
- When used with thermal underclothing good thermal protection is provided both in and out of water.
- Short suit-drying time.
- Loose fitting provides comfort and mobility.
- Some drag is created underwater.
- Can be expensive.
- If holed it may fill with water, losing all thermal protection. It can be very difficult to exit the water with a flooded suit.

Figure 23 A diver preparing equipment in a Membrane Drysuit

Figure 24 Semi-Drysuit

Neoprene Drysuit
- Closed-cell expanded foam neoprene. Shoulder or across-body waterproof zip and integral boots.
- Majority of neoprene drysuits are fitted with neoprene wrist/neck seals.
- Inherently buoyant suit. Similar to semi-dry suit the buoyancy will vary with depth as the material becomes compressed
- Good thermal protection in and out of the water.
- After use the neoprene drysuit may take some time to fully dry.
- Durable and hard wearing.
- Maintains some thermal protection if flooded, but still difficult to exit the water.

Neoprene Drysuit (Crushed or compressed)
- Compressed or crushed expanded foam neoprene. As the neoprene is crushed during the manufacturing process it does not suffer the effects of material compression like standard neoprene.
- Reduced inherent buoyancy.
- Good thermal protection in and out of the water.
- After use the neoprene drysuit may take some time to fully dry.
- Durable and hard wearing.
- Maintains some thermal protection if flooded, but still difficult to exit the water.

Figure 25 Neoprene Drysuit

The Aqualung

The 'aqualung' or SCUBA (an acronym for **S**elf-**C**ontained **U**nderwater **B**reathing **A**pparatus) is the principal equipment with which safe underwater breathing may be carried out. Its invention is credited to the late diving pioneer, Jacques Cousteau, who developed apparatus for self-contained underwater breathing in the late 1940s. The equipment comprises three main pieces: a high-pressure cylinder, a regulator generally referred to as a "demand valve", and a buoyancy compensator.

Cylinders

The cylinder is our very own self-contained air supply. Cylinders store compressed air at extremely high pressure. To give an idea of the pressures involved, a bus tyre is filled to approximately 10 bar, whilst a dive cylinder is pressurised to between 232 bar and 300 bar. Due to the high pressures present within a cylinder, great care must be taken when handling and storing diving cylinders. The metal dive cylinder is filled with pure breathing air and not just oxygen as many journalists often report as being the gas that divers use.

Cylinder sizes are normally measured in water capacity (litres). Normal cylinder sizes are 10-12 & 15 litres for single cylinders. Smaller cylinders come in 2-3 litre form for reserve air or stage decompression stops. The quantity of air that would fill an average telephone box is the approximate amount which when compressed would fill a 12-litre cylinder.

Cylinders can be twinned for divers wanting to make up a set for deep diving. These are known as a twinset and are normally joined together using a manifold. Twinsets that are connected together using an isolating manifold allow the use of two completely independent regulators, providing the added advantage of additional safety.

Figure 26 A selection of diving cylinders

Figure 27 Manifold used to couple cylinder twinsets

Cylinders are available in either aluminium or steel construction. Steel cylinders have a curved base and thin walls of 4-5 mm thickness. Aluminium alloy cylinders have a flat base and are made with thicker walls consisting of around 11 mm. Thicker walls are necessary because of the softer metals from which they are made. For the same comparative cylinder capacity, the steel cylinder will probably be lighter. Out of the water cylinders weigh between 10 and 16 kg however once in the water the diver will notice they feel almost weightless. Aluminium cylinders become positively buoyant when empty – steel cylinders do not.

All cylinders are fitted with rubber boots. High-pressure cylinders should never be left stood up unattended. Protective covers are available to protect them from getting scratched, covers come in plastic or heavy-duty nylon in a variety of colours. The official cylinder colour for compressed air diving cylinders is grey with a black and white quartered top shoulder, although manufacturers supply cylinders normally in white or yellow.

Cylinder markings
When buying a cylinder it is important to inspect markings that are stamped on to the cylinder. The markings ensure that the cylinder is approved and suitable for underwater use. The cylinder markings should be left clearly visible and must not be painted over.
Markings to look for include:
- Water Capacity (WC) = cylinder size
- Working Pressure (WP)
- Test Pressure (TP)
- Serial Number
- Weight
- Date of Manufacture
- Test Date (British standard or CE Mark)

Figure 28 Common cylinder markings

Steel cylinders
The cylinder is coated from new and if well maintained should not rust. It is important to ensure that you get your air fills from a reputable

filling station. A series of wet fills will soon start the rust cycle within the cylinder.

Aluminium alloy
Although the cylinder does not rust it will still corrode. Earlier cylinders had problems with the screw threads stretching, ultimately reducing the life of the cylinder.

Regulations
To ensure that the cylinder meets British requirements as a diving cylinder there are two regulations governing the manufacture of cylinders. These regulations are:
   BS 5045 Part 1 (steel cylinders)
   BS 5045 Part 3 (alloy cylinders)

Earlier specifications include HOT, HOL, IWKA. Cylinders with these specifications are now largely being discarded when as they fail to meet modern testing standards.

Testing/Inspection
It is a legal requirement that all diving cylinders are tested every two years. If the cylinder passes the test, the test date will be stamped on the cylinder. If the cylinder fails the test it must be destroyed. It is illegal (and dangerous) to fill a cylinder, which is out of test.

Cylinders must be visually inspected every two years from the date of manufacture and hydraulically tested every four years. Cylinder testing should only be carried out by suitably qualified persons, at a special test station suitably equipped. To ensure that test stations and testing personnel remain up to the task it was thought necessary to set up an independent watchdog. The Inspectorate for Diving Equipment Servicing and Testing (IDEST) was formed to oversee this assignment. IDEST currently enjoys the support of UK diving agencies, along with many manufacturers/ distributors. With acknowledgement from the HSE the organisation continues to enjoy increasing growth.

In order to be certified as an approved IDEST testing facility stations are visited to ensure they meet set standards for servicing and testing. Stations are re-inspected at set intervals to ensure that standards remain current. Non-IDEST test stations are not inspected and can/may set their own standards. There are currently over 50 IDEST stations.

In a visual inspection, the cylinder is inspected internally and externally for damage, scores, pitting, corrosion and thread damage, all of which can cause failure. Special cleaning processes may remove light corrosion.

Compressed air is no longer the only gas used for diving, it is important to note that when choosing a diving cylinder its use is restricted to the gas it was originally purchased for, unless the cylinder is specially cleaned. Any cylinder that is going to be used for Nitrox (EANx) must be cleaned annually for the higher oxygen content. Once cleaned and serviced the cylinder is in 'oxygen service'. Only cylinders in oxygen service can be filled with Nitrox. Once cleaned and filled with Nitrox the cylinder should not be used for standard compressed air. If standard compressed air is all that is available an additional filter is required to double filter the air prior to entering the Nitrox cylinder. If this is undertaken the oxygen service of the cylinder is not affected. Cylinders, which are used for Nitrox diving, are commonly painted yellow in colour and have a green and yellow sticker across the middle indicating its dedication to nitrox use. There are moves from the EU to re classify cylinder colourations and some Nitrox cylinders may not be yellow and have a Black and White sticker to indicate they are in Oxygen service and can be used for Nitrox.

Figure 29 A cylinder being tested

The hydraulic test consists of measuring the cylinder diameter when empty, filling it with water and then hydraulically pumping it up to its Test Pressure. The expansion of the cylinder is measured. When the pressure is released the expansion should return to normal. If the permanent expansion is more than 5% of the diameter, the cylinder will fail the test.

Satisfactory performance in all aspects of the test means that the cylinder is fit for further use and it will be issued with a test certificate and the shoulder of the cylinder will be stamped with the date of test and the test house stamp. BS 5430 regulations require that the test house destroy any cylinder that fails the test.

Steel cylinders are more prone to test failure due to corrosion as they suffer from a progressive rusting process. Aluminium cylinders are affected by oxidation, which results in the formation of a coating that can camouflage the corrosive action. Aluminium is a softer material than steel and, consequently, is more prone to superficial damage. First-stage cylinder, or pillar, valves are normally made of brass that can corrode into the aluminium, due to electrolytic action. This can cause seizure of the valve in the cylinder threads unless it is periodically removed and cleaned.

The capacity, working pressure and material used in manufacture classify a cylinder. Working Pressure (WP) is the operational pressure of the cylinder, measured in Bar. Cylinders usually have working pressures in the range 150-232 Bar, newer cylinders can take up to 300 Bar. Cylinder capacities range from 0.7L (emergency BCD cylinder) to 18L (extra large main diving cylinder). To get sufficient air into a dive cylinder a compressor that provides pure breathing air is used. The air goes through an intricate process of filters and filter materials in an effort to make it pure enough to breathe underwater. These filters dry the air before removing any oil. There are strict requirements regarding the amount of contaminants allowed in breathing air.

Figure 30 A dive cylinder compressor

Cylinder valve

The cross flow cylinder valve has now largely superseded the older style 'cylinder pillar valve'. Cross flow valves are screwed into the cylinder neck with a parallel thread, sealed with an O-ring, whilst the pillar valve has a taper thread, which is sealed with PTFE tape. Both valves are opened and closed like a water tap i.e. anti-clockwise opens the valve and clockwise closes it. An outer O-ring is used to form a seal on A-clamp cylinder valves (so called from the shape of the clamp that fits on the valve) so that an A-clamp diving regulator can be connected to it.

Figure 31 Cylinder pillar valve

It is advised that cylinders used with higher pressures than 232 bar (300 bar) use the screw type DIN clamp. The O-ring on a DIN cylinder valve is inside the mating surfaces and requires a DIN fitting type of regulator. The O-ring on either cylinder valve should be inspected prior to fitting the regulator.

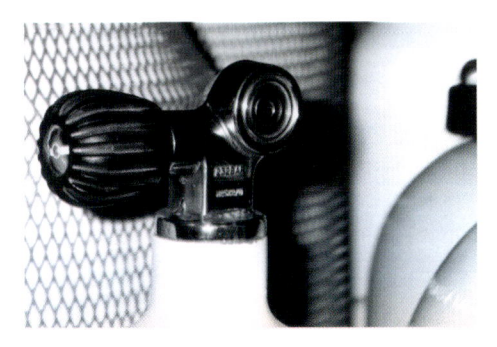

Figure 32 Cross flow A-Clamp cylinder valve

Figure 33 Cross flow DIN cylinder valve

All valves have an anti-debris tube, which extends deep into the cylinder and so prevents dust, rust etc. from reaching the valve mechanism should the cylinder become inverted.

Most cross flow cylinder valves can be used as an A-clamp or DIN fitting. The screw DIN fitting is the standard connection in some countries, so when travelling abroad it is important to establish what type of cylinder fittings are employed if it is intended to use a UK-pattern regulator.

In operation the cylinder valves should be opened almost fully anticlockwise; when closing the valve excessive force should not be used as this can damage the plastic valve seat. If there is any stiffness in the operation of the valve or it fails to turn off or on properly, then a suitably qualified person should inspect the cylinder.

Compressed air is no longer the only gas used for diving, it is important to note that when choosing a diving cylinder its use is restricted to the gas it was originally purchased for, unless the cylinder is specially cleaned. Any cylinder that is going to be used for nitrox (EANx) must be cleaned for the higher oxygen content (oxygen clean). Once cleaned and filled with nitrox the cylinder should not be used for standard compressed air. Cylinders which are used for nitrox diving, are painted yellow in colour and should have a green band across the middle indicating their dedication to nitrox use.

The Regulator
First Stage
The first stage is typically thought of as a pressure-reducing valve. The first stage of the regulator is attached to the cylinder via a clamp (A-clamp) or a DIN fitting. The first stage is normally constructed from chrome-plated brass.

Figure 34 Complete regulator

Figure 35 Regulator A-Clamp and DIN fitting

In a 'balanced' demand valve both ends of the valve stem are exposed to intermediate pressure air. This results in less force being exerted on the valve stem as it is returned to the seat. Water, at ambient pressure, pushes the valve away from its seat as the diver inhales, so allowing air to pass through. This configuration is fail-safe by design and consequently modern regulators of this type are highly reliable. In case of a component failure, the system would revert to free-flow operation (i.e. continuous air).

When the diver inhales, the pressure in the first stage allows the pressure to drop to around 8 - 10 bars above ambient water pressure. To achieve this, the diaphragm or a piston comes into contact with the surrounding water. The first stage has various ports on it from which various connections can be attached, one of which is a high-pressure port for a pressure gauge. This port is unaffected by the reducing effect of the first stage and therefore gives an accurate reading of the cylinder's pressure.

Other connections include:
- An alternative air source for emergencies
- Dry suit inflation hose
- Buoyancy Compensator inflation hose.

Second Stage (the Demand Valve)

The second stage is the part that contains the breathing mechanism and is made of a lightweight durable material (e.g. plastic). Both valves operate in relation to the ambient pressure and the pressure downstream of the valve. The demand valve provides air at the correct pressure to the diver at any depth.

The demand valve supplies air to the diver on demand (i.e. when required). Breathing in opens the small seat to allow air in, whilst breathing out shuts the valve off saving air. This is operated simply by inhaling. If the demand valve is removed from the mouth underwater it will fill with water, which must be expelled before the diver can breathe from it again. For this reason each demand valve is equipped with a purge button that may be depressed to manually open the air inlet valve. This should be used to test the

Figure 36 Demand valve

device prior to diving and for expelling any air left in the system before removing the regulator at the end of the day's diving.

The diver should also expel water and debris from inside the second stage and relieve the inter-stage pressure prior to disassembly of the aqualung. The exhaust valve location varies with different regulator types, but is conventionally at the bottom of the mouthpiece and angled away from the diver's field of vision.

As the regulator is an essential piece of equipment the diver should choose wisely (some regulators are not suitable for cold water).

The Buoyancy Compensator

The buoyancy compensator is not just fitted to help carry the cylinder. The buoyancy compensator can be a vital piece of lifesaving equipment. The buoyancy compensator is used to help compensate for the water pressure compression of any air filled spaces within diving suits, and body air spaces. This is achieved by injecting the appropriate amount of air into the compensator. It is important to remember that any injected air will expand upon ascent.

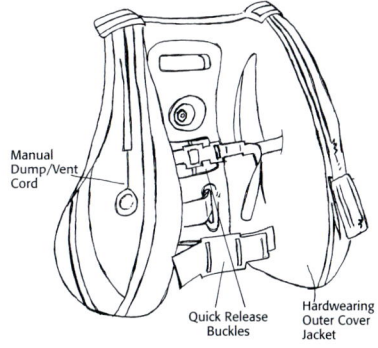

Figure 37 Buoyancy compensator attributes

Figure 38 Buoyancy compensator

Dry suit divers can use dry suit inflation on descent to help prevent or compensate for any suit compression (squeeze). Care should be taken to choose the correct size and amount of buoyancy offered. All buoyancy compensators must have a direct feed mechanism, which is supplied with air from the first stage of the regulator for routine buoyancy adjustment. Whichever system is selected it should provide enough buoyancy to stay afloat at the surface or to give emergency buoyancy whilst rescuing or being rescued.

Some experienced deep divers prefer the type of buoyancy compensator that keeps all the buoyancy at the rear of the diver - these types are known as 'wings' or technical jackets. These are preferred as they keep the diver's front clear. The buoyancy compensator is fitted with a collection of 'D' rings, which can be used for clipping on accessories such as cameras and torches. When choosing the right BC the diver should consider what type of diving they intend doing, as there are jackets designed for different purposes. Some buoyancy compensators are only capable of carrying single cylinders and cannot carry twinsets.

Some buoyancy compensators are primarily aimed at the travelling diver. This type of jacket is best suited to tropical waters where the diver is likely to be wearing a thinner diving suit. These types of buoyancy compensator will not provide much underwater lift (buoyancy) for a fully equipped UK diver. The diver would be better going for a buoyancy compensator which has an inner bag (bladder) and additional lift to meet the demanding conditions that prevail at some UK dive sites.

Most buoyancy jackets use a webbing 'cam' band for securing the cylinder, whilst some jackets utilise metal bands for securing the cylinder. All buoyancy compensators are equipped with direct feed systems for inflating the jacket, consisting of a low-pressure hose fed from the regulator first stage. To inflate the jacket all that is required is a simple push of a button. Some jackets are equipped with a direct feed that also incorporates an emergency demand valve.

There are some buoyancy compensators that come equipped with a small (1.5 litre) emergency back up cylinder. The cylinder is filled from the diver's main cylinder. One of the dangers of this system is that whilst the diver has his main diving cylinder(s) tested few divers bother having the emergency cylinder tested. The ideal solution is to have them tested like normal compressed air cylinders. Careful use is recommended in emergency situations only, as they are capable of inflating the jacket rapidly, resulting in an accelerated rate of ascent. The preferred option for inflating BCs is the direct feed method, which is both safe and controlled.

It is important to ensure that the working pressure of an emergency cylinder is compatible with the working pressure of the aqualung cylinder. Emergency BC cylinders should not be filled from cylinders containing nitrox (EANx) mixtures, unless they too have been prepared for use with nitrox.

Although not very common, there are some jackets that are equipped with a CO_2 cartridge for inflation. These are not recommended as they can only be used once. If during an ascent too much is vented there is no way of replenishing it. They can suffer badly from corrosion due to the nature of their manufacture, making them unreliable.

Apart from choice of colour choosing the right buoyancy compensator is dependent on choosing the correct size and preferred style. The fit should be comfortable whilst inflated just as much as when it is deflated. The controls should be easy to locate and operate.

Gauges
Pressure/contents gauge
One of the most important pieces of a diver's equipment is the pressure gauge. The gauge allows the diver to see how much air remains in

the cylinder. The pressure gauge connects to the first stage of the diver's regulator, through one of the high-pressure ports.

Most pressure/contents gauges come as a single unit attached to the regulator or in a console incorporating other gauges.

Depth gauge
In order to calculate decompression schedules and safely manage them the diver must be able to determine his depth during any part of the dive. To facilitate this the diver must be equipped with a depth gauge. Common gauges are all fitted with maximum depth indicator needle. This is an additional needle, which gets pushed round as the diver descends. As the diver ascends this needle will stay at the maximum depth attained, allowing the diver to see what maximum was reached during the dive.

Figure 39 Assorted gauges

Diving watch

As well as knowing how deep they go the diver must know what duration has been spent at the maximum depth. A diving watch is required to complement the depth gauge. It is important to choose a watch that is not only waterproof, but also able to withstand the pressure at depth. An alternative to a watch, used in many cases is the 'dive timer' or computer (see Chapter 10).

Torches

Even during the best of conditions a torch is best carried. It may just be to look under small overhangs, or illuminate and correct the colour loss at depth. It is, however, a safety item of equipment and one few divers go without. Torches are available as large lanterns right down to small models that attach to the mask. They also come in a variety of power options and brightness, with either rechargeable or disposable batteries.

Figure 42 Powerful torch

Figure 40 Divers watch

Figure 41 Dive light selection

Surface marker buoys and reels (SMB)

The surface marker buoy is a surface float towed during the dive by the diver connected to a reel. One of its uses is to show the position of the diver throughout the dive. The safety cover can use the line to communicate with the divers in an emergency. The chosen type of float should be conspicuous. Any float which blends in with the surrounding water will be hard to see by the surface cover.

Figure 43 Surface Marker Buoy

Figure 44 Delayed Surface Marker Buoy

As well as the surface marker buoy the reel is a useful addition to a diver's equipment. The diver can use a reel by clipping onto the anchor or shot line at the start of the dive and reeling line out during the dive. At the agreed time of return the diver turns around and simply starts reeling back to the original starting point, where a safe ascent can be made.

Figure 45 Divers Reels

Maintenance of diving equipment

Equipment maintenance means maintaining all diving equipment in a safe working condition. If equipment is not looked after then it increases the risks of equipment failure, possibly at the wrong time (if any time is the right time?). Maintenance involves:
- Cleaning
- Repair and Maintenance
- Correct Storage

Diving equipment is regularly submerged in salt water, so unless it is properly cleaned, maintained and stored, it will start to decay or rust and become unsafe. Chlorinated water, as in the swimming pool, or dirty freshwater will have a similar effect. Equipment maintenance is therefore necessary to:
- Keep the equipment in safe working order.
- Prolong its operational lifetime.

Avoid exposure to hydrocarbons such as oil, petrol, grease, suntan lotion etc. Avoid contact with underwater obstacles (e.g. abrasive rocks, wrecks etc.) and sand/grit.

After every dive wash in plenty of clean fresh water to:
- Prevent salt building up
- Remove sand and grit
- Allow to air dry
- When dry, store in a cool dry place, preferably in darkness (silicon decomposes in sunlight).

After every few dives:
- Perform regular visual inspection and check:
- Generally for signs of wear and damage.
- Rubber straps and hoses for sign of perishing ('cracking' effect)
- Webbing and suit seals for signs of fraying.
- Buckles for correct operation.

Specific equipment maintenance
Semi-Drysuits and Wetsuits
- Wash suit inside and out in fresh water.
- Dry the suit completely, avoiding direct sunlight.
- Clean and lubricate zips.
- Examine the suit regularly for tears and damage.
- If possible, avoid folding – hang like a drysuit, or lie flat.

Drysuits
- Close zip and wash outside of suit after every dive.
- Check all seams and seals regularly for deterioration.
- Dust neck and wrist seals with talc after rinsing and drying.
- Keep the zip clean and lubricated, using beeswax or special zip cleaner/lubricant.
- Check inflation/venting valves for correct operation.
- Avoid contact with hydrocarbons, which cause perishing of seals
- Avoid folding the suit, especially zips, during storage. Hang on a padded hanger or store as directed by the manufacturer.

Cylinders
- The outside of the cylinder should be rinsed in clean, fresh water after use.
- The cylinder valve may be momentarily opened to discharge any water from the air outlet point. Never store cylinders empty, as this will allow corrosion to flourish. A pressure level of 50 Bar is adequate.
- Cylinders should be stored in an upright position.
- Inspect the O-ring regularly and replace if it shows any sign of damage. A webbing or neoprene cover will prevent damage to the external finish of the cylinder.
- Whilst transporting cylinders, care should be taken not to damage the outer surface in any way, through improper handling or movement during carriage.

Regulators
The regulator is an essential piece of life-support equipment and, consequently, it is imperative that is maintained in first-rate condition. Avoid dropping it or placing in sand etc. It must be

rinsed carefully with clean, fresh water after first replacing the dust cap cover over the first stage inlet when the regulator is removed from cylinder. Air from the cylinder should not be used to blow away water and debris from this inlet, prior to fitting the dust cap, and care should be taken to ensure debris or water does not enter the first stage. The purge button must not be depressed when rinsing an un-pressurised regulator.

It is highly imperative that a specialist technician services the regulator at regular intervals (annually for a regulator in active use). HP and IP/LP outlet hoses should be inspected periodically and replaced if they show any signs of damage, bulging or perishing.

Hose protectors are useful in protecting the metal unions at the hose ends and to reduce the amount of bending at these places. Check carefully for damage to hoses, mouthpieces and direct feed connections.

Buoyancy Compensators (BCs)
- After use rinse the inside as well as outside with clean fresh water.
- Periodically rinse the inside with a weak disinfectant solution to kill any bacteria.
- Check for leaks before and after every dive.
- Re-grease the purge button on the Emergency Air Cylinder after every 10 or so dives using only silicon grease.
- Inspect webbing regularly for damage e.g. caused by the weightbelt rubbing.

Torches
- If using rechargeable batteries, follow the recommended maintenance schedule.
- Apply silicon grease to O-ring on a regular basis.
- Do not use for extended periods of time out of water.
- Inspect lanyard for any chaffing.

Conclusions
Maintaining all items of diving equipment is essential to ensure safety. Equipment should be washed in clean fresh water after every dive, then air-dried and stored away from direct sunlight. Follow appropriate maintenance/service schedules.

Chapter 4 Practical Diver Training

After completing a basic swimming test you are ready to move on to using basic equipment. Your first experiences will normally be in the shallow end of a swimming pool where you can get accustomed to using the equipment comfortably and safely.

Water Entry Methods

There are various methods for entering the water and the actual techniques used will depend on the lesson being undertaken and your instructor's preferences. Some instructors may choose to have you sit on the pool side and fit the scuba set allowing you to make a controlled seated entry to the water, whilst other instructors prefer to put the aqualung set on the individual once they are standing in the shallow end.

It is likely that after your first session entry to the water will be made by using the steps, wearing the

Figure 46 Giant stride entry

aqualung after first placing the basic equipment on the poolside. An alternative method and one used as a progressive move is by making a stride entry. When making a stride entry you should partially inflate the BC, and place one hand over the mask and regulator (this will stop them being displaced as you enter the water) before stepping over the edge of the pool.

If the diver is carrying any equipment or cameras then the preferred water entry method will be a forward roll entry. To make safe entry the diver should tuck any loose items in by holding them close. After inflating your buoyancy compensator, bend your legs at the knees, and then lower your face to your chest. It is advisable to place one hand over your middle; this will stop your gauges from swinging up into your face. Before making a gentle forward roll you can still hold one hand over your mask and regulator. It is important to avoid any forced jump when completing a forward roll.

Before making any sort of entry the golden rule is to make sure that you can get out when ready. You should always check to make sure it is safe to enter the water, there should be no obstructions, including other divers or rocks.

Snorkel
A snorkel will fill up with water if the open end is permitted to go under the water. Although most snorkels have drainage valves, all divers should practise this skill using a snorkel without a valve, so that they can cope with basic snorkels. The diver must be able to competently clear this flooded water. In order to clear a flooded snorkel a short sharp blow through the mouthpiece is all that is required. To begin with, whilst standing in the shallow end place your mouth underwater to get accustomed to breathing through a snorkel.

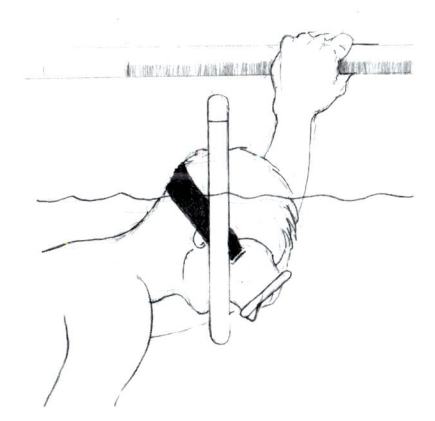

Figure 47 Poolside static snorkel practice

Mask and Snorkel
To progress fit the snorkel to the mask using the retaining ring supplied with the snorkel. At the poolside it is essential to prepare the mask by rubbing a coating of saliva or one of the commercially available anti-mist solutions over the inside of the glass whilst it is dry. Rinsing the mask will then stop it misting up during use. The mask should be fitted to the face making sure no hair is trapped between the skirt and your skin (this will allow water to enter). The straps should be adjusted, so that the mask is firm without being too tight or too slack. This is a good time to check for any leaks. You will be encouraged at this stage to practise snorkel clearing with your mask on: simply lower your face into the water with the snorkel in place and allow it to flood. The angle of the snorkel should be adjusted so it fits comfortably at the correct angle.

Displacement snorkel clearing
Displacement clearing is an alternative method of clearing a flooded snorkel. As you ascend you should already be looking towards the surface. In this position with the head tilted back the open end of the snorkel should be lower than the mouthpiece. You should exhale a little air into the snorkel as you ascend. As you continue to ascend the excess air will expand displacing the water. As you surface continue to exhale through the snorkel. When you bring your head

forward the snorkel should be empty and there will be no need for the short sharp blow.

Mask clearing

Even the best fitting mask may eventually let some water in: clearing this water is a simple skill. If water enters the mask, on the surface, it can be cleared by simply lifting the mask so water is allowed to drain from the bottom.

For masks with a purge valve, all that is required is for the diver to look down whilst exhaling through the nose. Where the mask has no purge valve, then the diver should press the top of the mask onto the forehead and then look upwards whilst exhaling through the nose. The air will have the effect of displacing any water. A steady exhalation is all that is required with either method. During pool training this skill is learnt by allowing the mask to partially flood before clearing it, the progression is then for fully flooding the mask before removing the mask altogether.

Figure 49 Mask clearing technique 2

Fins

Fins for use in the pool are called slipper fins. They are worn without boots and do not have the adjusting straps of open water fins. The poolside should be used for stability when fitting fins. Always wet both feet and fin foot compartment for fitting slipper fins. Walking with fins on is easier and safer when walking backwards or sideways. The diver should avoid walking with fins on out of the water. This may help avoid embarrassing or painful falls.

After fitting basic equipment the next step is to become proficient in using it. Mastering the use of basic equipment is the right progressive step to making future diver training easier.

Surface finning

Holding the poolside, with your face down (mask and snorkel in place), stretch legs out on the surface. Finning legs almost straight, the action should come from the hips. It is

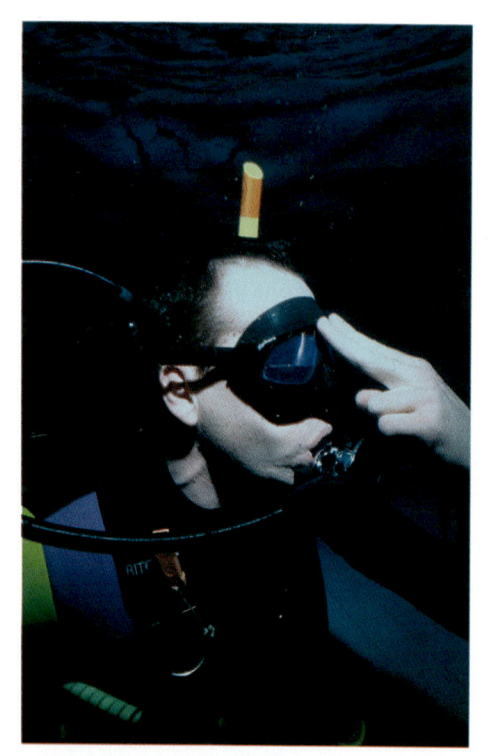

Figure 48 Mask clearing technique 1

important to avoid any excess bending of the knees (cycle action). This requires extra energy without providing any additional propulsion.

Once your instructor is satisfied with your finning action, you can progress to finning round on the surface. It is easier to develop a good finning action from the beginning rather than trying to correct it at a later stage. Finning on the surface or under the water, arms should be kept near to the body.

Figure 50 Correct surface finning technique

Surface dives

A surface dive is the easiest method used to get below the water. The aim of a surface dive is to dive below the surface with the minimum of effort. A surface dive can be broken down into simple clear stages:
- Lying horizontal on the surface, bend the body at the waist.
- With arms pointing straight down, lift your legs so they are clear of the water and vertical above you, so their weight can help drive you down.
- Pull down with your arms as the weight of your body propels you down.
- Keep your legs together and do not use them until you are fully submerged. Thrashing your fins on the surface serves no purpose.
- Once clear of the surface the diver can come to a horizontal position by using his arms and gently bending his body.

Figure 51 Three stages of a surface dive

Feet first dive

A variation of the surface dive is the feet first dive;
- In a vertical position, fin slightly upwards.
- Allow yourself to sink with your arms above your head. As you submerge use your arms to pull yourself under.
- Once underwater you can bend over to get into a head down position.

Surfacing drill

Some simple guidelines should be followed when making any ascent. These become essential when diving in open water.
- At the agreed time both divers should signal that they are going to ascend.
- Divers should be in control of buoyancy so all that is required is for them to start finning up.
- Both divers should ascend face to face.
- In the final few metres it is important to turn through 360 degrees to ensure there are no obstacles nearby. Whilst doing this you should extend one arm over your head for protection.
- As you surface you should again turn round in a full circle to make sure there are no oncoming vessels approaching. You should be able to dive quickly back down should it be necessary.

- Once you are satisfied everything is okay you should inflate your buoyancy compensator.
- It is very important to control the rate of any ascents to avoid any possible injuries.

During all these skills your instructor will guide and assist you to develop good techniques.

Scuba divers always descend and ascend together and remain together underwater, usually in pairs. Diving with a partner, called a 'buddy', provides mutual enjoyment in a shared experience, and mutual help if anything goes wrong. A snorkel or free diver dives down singly, allowing the buddy to keep watch at the surface for approaching boats. In the event of an underwater problem, the buddy at the surface is able to provide assistance to the submerged diver, as he will be ready to go down again.

Diving Signals

To establish underwater communications the diver will have to resort to hand signals. There is a range of signals each with its own definition that can be used. Diving signals should always be given clearly: it may be necessary to repeat the signal to confirm understanding.

Signals can be divided into two different categories:
- Underwater diver to diver signals.
- Diver to surface/shore cover signals.

Diver to Diver signals

Throughout the dive the divers use signals to communicate on aspects of the dive. Before giving a signal it is important to gain the attention of the buddy. It is useless giving a signal and

Something wrong

Stop

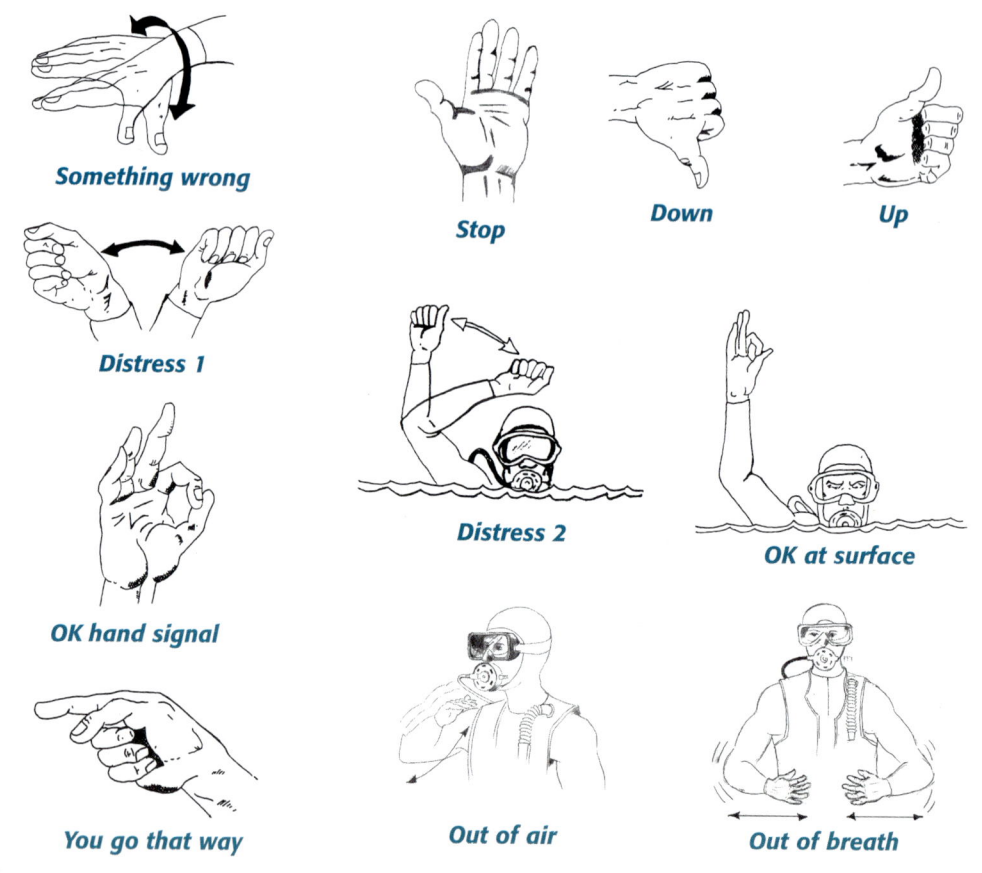

Down

Up

Distress 1

Distress 2

OK at surface

OK hand signal

You go that way

Out of air

Out of breath

Figure 52 Diving signals

expecting a reply if your buddy is looking another way and didn't see you signal him.

It is very important that once a signal is given an acknowledgement is received. If an okay signal is given with no reply the diver giving the signal may assume something is wrong and act accordingly.

Diver to Surface/Shore Cover
The diver and safety cover use signals to communicate with each other. After entering the water from a boat the diver should signal okay to both the boatman and his buddy. This would tell the boatman that everything is okay and it is clear for the buddy to enter. At the end of a dive an okay signal from the divers to the boatman signifies things are fine. When giving signals from a distance the signals are the same, but given with the arm raised, to make the signal more prominent.

Night diving signals
Being able to communicate underwater efficiently is even more important during night diving activities or during dives with limited underwater visibility. The signals used are the same and they are given in just the same way with the exception that the diver uses a torch to illuminate the hand signal. The diver should gain the attention of his buddy before giving a signal. The easiest way of doing this is to shine the torch beam slowly from side-to-side in front of the other diver. Once you have their attention you can illuminate your hand to give the signal and wait for a reply. When using the torch for signalling it is important to illuminate just the signal and avoid shining the light into your buddy's face. This will destroy his night vision for several minutes.

Once you have the aqualung equipment and have mastered using basic equipment, your next step is to move onto aqualung diving skills. These skills will help prepare you for open water diving and are skills that even experienced divers will practise from time to time.

Buoyancy control
Being able to adjust your buoyancy at the touch of a button is essential to safe open water diving. Divers who do not adequately control their buoyancy can find themselves floating up towards the surface during the dive, or damaging fragile marine life such as corals by landing on them. The diver who constantly hits the bottom will also soon find themselves in poor visibility.

Neutral buoyancy is a term used to describe a state where the diver neither sinks down nor floats up. Good buoyancy control is only achieved by plenty of practice. During early training the diver will become accustomed to weight adjusted on the belt until they are capable of controlling buoyancy. When using the buoyancy compensator for routine adjustment it is best to get into a pattern of small bursts of air rather than holding the inflator button down.

The fin pivot is a good technique of practising neutral buoyancy. Lie face down on the bottom, breathing slowly and deeply. Add small amounts of air into the buoyancy compensator until you reach a point where you slowly pivot upwards on your fins as you inhale. As you exhale if you are neutrally buoyant you should slowly pivot downwards.

Figure 53 Buoyancy control / Fin pivot

Regulator Clearing/recovery

If the regulator (demand valve) is removed or knocked out of the mouth underwater it will fill with water. It is essential that every diver is capable of replacing the regulator and clearing the water before taking their next breath. This is the core skill used if you are forced to share a demand valve in an out-of-air situation. There are two basic methods of clearing a flooded demand valve, these are using exhaled air and using the purge button.

When replacing the demand valve, if you have enough air in your lungs all that is required is a short sharp blow into the regulator as it is replaced. In most cases this will dispel any water through the exhaust diaphragm. If you have no remaining air then you will have to use the purge button as the regulator is replaced. The button is depressed as the demand valve is replaced; the flow of air will force out any water. The first breath should be taken cautiously in case of any residual water.

This can be safely practised in the pool. On the bottom, take a deep breath, and remove your mouthpiece. If the mouthpiece begins to bubble briefly turn the mouthpiece so that it faces downwards. You can use one of the methods described above to replace the demand valve. Whenever you practise any form of regulator removal you should gently exhale a continuous steady stream of bubbles, this gives an indication that you are not holding your breath.

Figure 54 Never hold your breath with regulator displaced

Regulator retrieval

If your demand valve accidentally comes out of your mouth you must be able to recover it. Recovering it can be done in many ways, one such method is the:

Arm sweep method - By tilting the body over to the right side, the demand valve should hang out. To retrieve the demand valve sweep your right arm down to your side and out in an arc. This should hook the hose, as the arm is raised the hose should be grabbed enabling you to replace the demand valve.

Figure 55 Regulator recovery one

Figure 56 Regulator recovery two

Free flowing regulator

In extreme cold circumstances there is an added risk of the regulator malfunctioning. It is possible that a demand valve may start to work on its own. This is referred to as a 'free flowing regulator'. A safety feature built into modern regulators known as a 'downstream valve' ensures that the flow of air will continue should there be a problem with the regulator. The regulators will supply the diver with air, although it may be at an increased rate (pressure). The diver simply carries on breathing, without totally sealing their lips round the mouthpiece. The escaping (excess) air will stop any water from entering the demand valve. Free flowing regulators are not a common problem, however the diver should be aware of how to deal with it.

Out-of-air situations

In the event that your air supply fails, or that of your buddy, you must be capable of dealing with the situation. There are a number of options available. Although not very commonly used these techniques should be practised by all divers, so that should the need arise the core skills will be there. Consideration should be given to the equipment configuration worn by each diver.

Alternative air source

This is the preferred method using the secondary demand valve (octopus). Each diver is advised to be equipped with such a device. In an out-of-air situation the appropriate signal should be given.

Both divers would approach each other, with the donor offering the octopus at eye level to the diver out of air. It is important to remain static momentarily so the diver without air can regain a comfortable breathing pattern. Once both divers are ready an ascent should be made. It is worth remembering that using this technique there will be two divers using the remaining air.

Figure 57 Divers Octopus

Figure 58 Diver giving the out-of-air signal

Figure 59 Alternative air source practice

Buddy breathing
If there is an out-of-air situation and the diver with air is not equipped with an alternative air source they will have to make an ascent sharing a single regulator. Divers are advised to perform a dry run on the surface. In the pool environment the divers practise this next to each other before moving apart. After giving the out of air signal both divers should approach each other. The donor of the regulator should take a deep breath before offering it to the diver out of air. The diver may require the use of the purge button, which should be kept clear.

Both divers should initially remain static to establish comfortable breathing. The rhythm for buddy breathing is to take two breaths each. Once both divers are ready, then they should proceed to the surface. Secure contact with each other is essential prior to starting the ascent.

It is not recommended to practice buddy breathing in open water.

Other forms of alternative air sources include:

Pony cylinder
A system favoured by some divers is the pony cylinder. The pony cylinder is normally around 3 litres, which is equipped with its own individual regulator. The cylinder is filled and tested just like normal dive cylinders.

BC Demand valve
Some buoyancy compensators are equipped with a power inflator that doubles as an emergency-breathing device. If the assisting diver has this system he would offer his own primary demand valve to the diver out of air, and use the power inflator device himself. One of the drawbacks with this type of system is that, in a possible volatile situation, you have to remove a perfectly good working demand valve and switch to the BC valve. The power inflator is generally fitted to the buoyancy compensator on a short hose and would not be long enough to reach another diver.

Figure 60 BC emergency demand valve

Twin Outlet Cylinder Valve
This is a special valve fitted to the top of the dive cylinder. It enables two completely different regulators to be used. This system is used in the same way that an octopus system works. The rate of air consumption would effectively increase as two divers utilise the remaining air. No matter what technique is used in an out-of-air situation it is a very tense period. A diver would not realise they are out of air until they go to inhale; it is then more than likely that they will approach you for air. They may will be in a state of extreme anxiety (panic), they may even go for the valve which they know is working: yours. Avoidance is better than the cure. The pool environment provides a good base for practice of out-of-air scenarios.

Equipment Removal/Replacement
It is unlikely that you will ever have to remove your equipment underwater, however there is a remote chance that you may become entangled in some way. Being able to effectively 'ditch and retrieve' your equipment can be a good booster to confidence should the need arise. Weightbelts should not be removed, as you will become positively buoyant which may lead to a rapid ascent. Practice in removal of equipment is advised at some stage. It is likely that you will have to remove equipment at the side of a boat. Removal of the scuba set underwater can be broken down into distinct stages. A good way to practise removing equipment is swapping scuba sets with a friend in a pool.

The first steps in removing equipment should be to kneel on the bottom. Start by dumping all the air from the buoyancy jacket. Loosen the buckles prior to unclipping them (the weightbelt is retained to provide stability).

The scuba set should be eased off the right shoulder whilst retaining the demand valve (continue breathing normally through the regulator). Move your scuba set around to position it in front of you.

Figure 61 A diver with equipment removed in a swimming pool

When you are both ready swim to the other scuba set. After recovering the demand valve you should be able to refit your buddy's equipment. This is a good way to become familiar with different equipment.

Chapter 5 Pressure, Physics and the Diver

Whenever divers descend they are affected by a number of changes. As they are not experienced in everyday life it is important the student understands the relevance of these changes. These changes will affect the diver to varying degrees, and will depend upon the actual dive being undertaken. Many of the changes can lead to serious consequences if they go unnoticed or are ignored.

Pressure

Air pressure is caused by the weight of air molecules in the atmosphere exerting a 'pressing' force. It is called atmospheric pressure and is measured in bars. In space, the absence of air means there is no pressure, thus it is 0 bar. The pressure gets higher and higher on approach of the earth's surface, such that at sea level the pressure is 1 bar (sometimes called 1 atmosphere or 1 atm). This is equivalent to 1 kg of force pressing down on every square centimetre of surface. This pressure does not cause any discomfort, as it is 'equalised' (or the same) in all of the air spaces in a human body.

Entering the sea and going deeper, the pressure is the combination of both the air and the water force, so it increases progressively. At 10 metres depth, the weight of water pressing on a body is equivalent to the pressure of the atmosphere at sea level. In other words, the pressure from 10 metres of water is equivalent to the pressure exerted by the whole atmosphere. Each 10 metres of water will result in another bar of pressure.

Altitude / depth	Pressure
Top of atmosphere	0 bar
Sea level	1 bar
10 metres	2 bar
20 metres	3 bar
30 metres	4 bar

In air and water, pressure acts in all directions, i.e. at 30m depth a body surface is subjected to a uniformly distributed pressure of 4 bar.

Measuring Pressure

When measuring pressure, instruments are normally related to atmospheric pressure i.e. a basic gauge reads zero when at a pressure of 1 bar. This is due to atmospheric pressure. The pressure gauge on a diving cylinder will read 200 bar, when it is actually 200 bar above atmospheric pressure: this is better known as gauge pressure. The real pressure is 201 bar. This is referred to as absolute pressure. In the table above, absolute pressure is used.

NB: Absolute Pressure = Gauge pressure + Atmospheric pressure.

Partial Pressure – Dalton's Law

Dalton's Law states that: *The total pressure of a gas is equal to the sum of partial pressure (pp), which each gas would have if it alone occupied the available space.*

Air at 1 bar pressure (figures rounded for calculations);
- Nitrogen = 80% of 1 bar = 0.8 bar
- Oxygen = 20% of 1 bar = 0.2 bar.

This is referred to as Partial Pressure, 'pp', and is an important component in scuba diving. The percentage of gases which make up air is the same throughout the breathable atmosphere, regardless of altitude. Although air in a scuba cylinder is compressed the percentage of the gases remains the same.

Partial Pressure is the pressure exerted by an individual gas, whether that gas is part of a mixture (as in air) or dissolved in a liquid (as in blood) or simply in any body tissue. Partial pressure is determined by the fraction of the gas in the mixture. Using Dalton's Law we can see that as air pressure increases or decreases, the partial pressure of each gas in a mix will do the same. As a diver descends the partial pressure exerted by each gas will also increase; conversely with any change in altitude (ascent) the partial pressure of gas will decrease.

Depth	Absolute Pressure	Partial Pressure O₂ (ppO₂)	Partial Pressure N₂ (ppN₂)	Volume
Surface	1 bar	0.2 bar	0.8 bar	One
10 metres	2 bar	0.4 bar	1.6 bar	Half
20 metres	3 bar	0.6 bar	2.4 bar	Third
30 metres	4 bar	0.8 bar	3.2 bar	Quarter

Table representing Dalton's Law.

Pressure and Volume – Boyle's Law

Boyle's Law states that: *Since all gases are compressible the volume they occupy will vary in direct proportion to any increase/decrease in pressure.*

This relationship between pressure and volume is fundamental to diving. The greater the pressure, the smaller the volume will be. Failure to recognise these effects may lead to pressure injuries.

Consider a balloon full of air, which has been blown up at sea level. If this balloon was taken on a dive, its size (volume) will decrease as it descends. During any ascent the balloon will return to its original size. If the balloon were taken up through the atmosphere, the pressure acting on it would decrease and our balloon would increase in size as the air within it expanded.

Displacement & Bouyancy - Archimedes' Principle

Any object submerged in water will receive an upthrust equal to the amount of water it displaces. An object that weighs less than the weight of liquid it displaces will float. This is

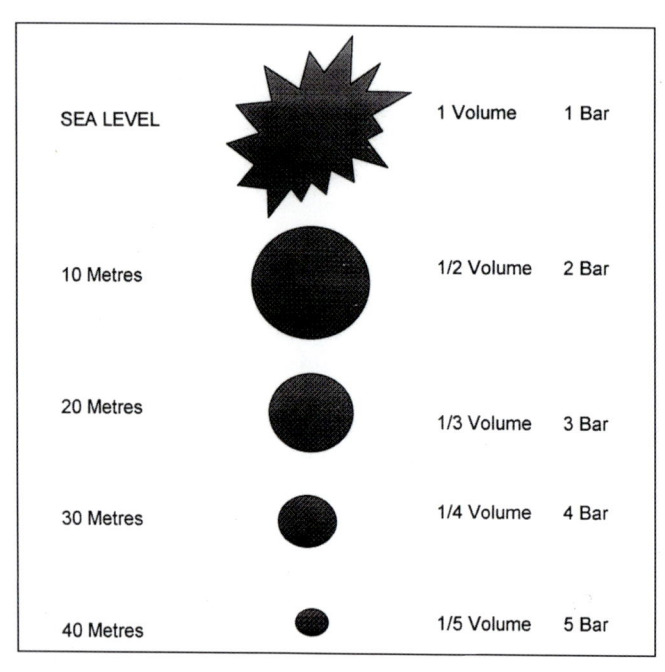

SEA LEVEL	1 Volume	1 Bar
10 Metres	1/2 Volume	2 Bar
20 Metres	1/3 Volume	3 Bar
30 Metres	1/4 Volume	4 Bar
40 Metres	1/5 Volume	5 Bar

Figure 62 Boyle's Law

known as positive buoyancy. If the weight of the object were greater than the weight of the liquid it displaces it would effectively sink. This is defined as negative buoyancy. To attain neutral buoyancy the object has a weight that is equal to the weight of water it displaces.

Temperature & Volume - Charles' Law

Charles' Law states that: *At a constant volume, the pressure of gas varies directly with absolute temperature.*

Air temperature can vary. Any gas that becomes heated will increase in volume and pressure if the amount of volume available is restricted. A typical example of this is an inflatable boat or diving cylinder that is left in direct sunlight. In the heat the pressure and hence volume will increase. In extreme cases the pressure may increase beyond normal working pressures and may cause failure of container.

Compared to Boyle's Law, Charles' Law is not as important for scuba divers because temperature underwater does not change enough to seriously affect air pressure in our cylinders.

Gas Absorption in liquids - Henry's Law

Henry's Law states that: *Where gas and liquid come into contact, gas will dissolve into the liquid until a level of saturation is reached, depending on the pressure exerted upon it.*

In the alveoli membrane air will dissolve into the bloodstream. The amount that dissolves depends on the partial pressure of the gas. As the diver descends the increased pressure will force more gas to dissolve. As the diver ascends the pressure decreases and any gas will be released from the liquid. A simple but effective way of demonstrating this is by inspecting a bottle of fizzy drink as it is opened. When the bottle is opened, the pressure of the gas above the liquid decreases and the carbon dioxide is allowed out of solution. If the bottle is opened in a controlled manner the rate of carbon dioxide is also controlled. The importance of

this controlled depressurisation can be related to the amount of gas that comes out of the diver's bloodstream during the ascent.

Carbon Dioxide in solution

Carbon Dioxide out of solution

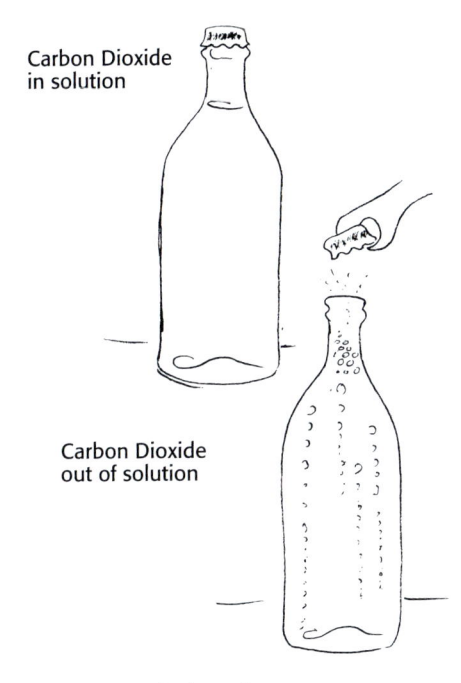

Figure 63 An example of Henry's Law

Air Spaces in the Human Body
Air is contained in the body in a variety of places, the main locations being:
- Sinuses
- Ears
- Air Spaces/Airways
- Lungs
- Stomach

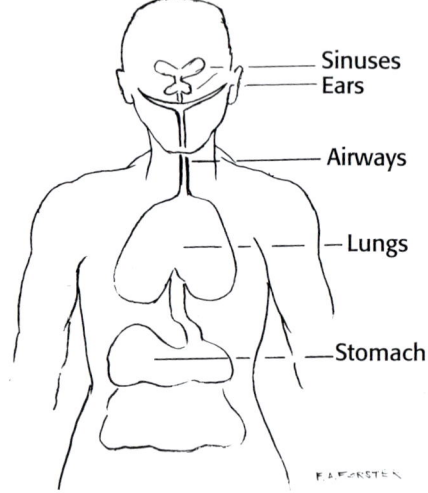

Figure 64 Body air spaces

The rest of the human body can be assumed to be either liquid or solid and is not affected by pressure to the same degree, although the diver uses artificial air spaces that are affected by pressure changes. These include;

- Masks
- Dry Suits
- Buoyancy Aids

The air within these air spaces must be controlled to help prevent the risk of injury. Boyle's Law affects any compressible airspace in the diver's body. As a diver descends, the increasing pressure will compress (squeeze) the air spaces in the body.

Sinuses
The sinuses are air-filled spaces inside the bone of the skull and are connected to the upper nasal passages. They exist to effectively reduce the weight of the skull and to protect against infection. Healthy sinuses will equalise pressure automatically. In the event of a cold or any kind of nasal infection, including hay fever or heavy catarrh, the passages connecting the sinuses (and ear) to the throat may become inflamed and may be clogged up or closed by mucus.
IF THIS IS THE CASE, DO NOT DIVE.

It is very unlikely that a diver with a cold will be able to properly equalise their sinuses during the descent and this will result in painful pressure damage (sinus barotrauma). Using decongestant medicines may help provide relief, however there is a risk that this relief may be temporary. The implications of such tablets wearing off prior to the conclusion of the dive should be fully considered. There is also the risk that, increased pressure may alter medication side effects with potentially serious consequences.

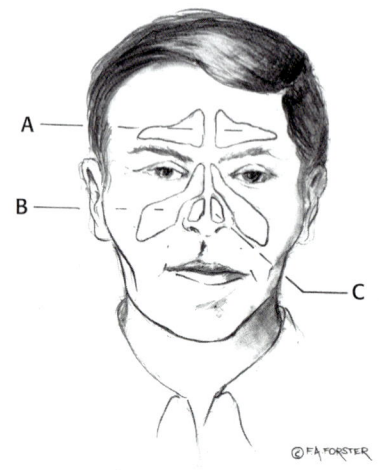

A = Frontal
B = Ethmoidal
C = Maxillary

Figure 65 The sinuses

Ears
The ears are divided into three parts: the outer ear, the middle ear, and the inner. The outer ear or auditory canal is an air-filled space, which is sealed off inside the ear at the eardrum. It is the eardrum that is most sensitive to increasing

pressure, as it is pushed inwards. It is essential that the diver takes immediate action to equalise the pressure in the ears, as damage to the eardrum can occur very easily (aural barotrauma). If the diver does not equalise this pressure, the eardrum will rupture allowing water to enter the middle ear. This will upset the diver's balance and hearing. A secondary problem would be the risk of allowing the ear to become infected. This would take some time to heal.

The middle ear is an air-filled space connected to the rear of the throat by the 'Eustachian Tube'. The inner ear is a fluid-filled space, which contains the three semi-circular canals. Although they play no part in hearing they are important as they control our balance.

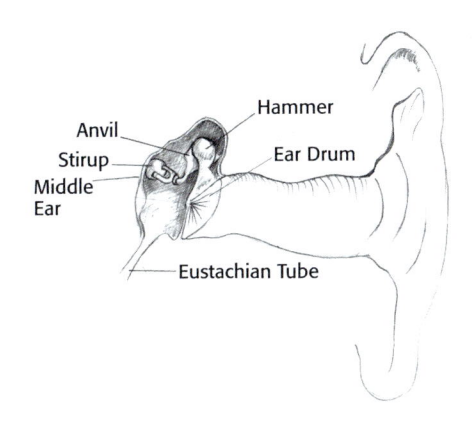

Figure 66 The ear

Equalisation methods
The most common method of equalising the ears is by using the 'Valsalva Manoeuvre': This is accomplished by pinching the nose, closing the mouth and blowing gently though the nose. Other ways of equalising the pressure are by swallowing, yawning or wiggling your jaw. It is important to start equalisation methods as soon as any descent is made. You should not wait for pain before acting. If the diver has trouble clearing his ears then he should stop the descent, ascend a little and then try again. A profound popping of the ears and feeling of pressure relief is a good indication of effective equalisation.

It is important to remember not to use excessive force when attempting to equalise the pressure, as it is possible to damage the eardrum. In the event that the ears will not clear, the only option is to abort the dive. Diving with a cold, nasal infection or any infection will impair successful equalisation. Ear-plugs should never be worn, as they effectively cause a pressure drop in the outer ear canal during descent. Tight fitting hoods may also cause similar problems as they prevent water at the same pressure of that surrounding the body to get to the ears. The airways/respiratory tract are flexible airways which, although affected by changes in pressure, will equalise automatically providing the diver breathes normally.

The Lungs
The body's respiratory system consists of the airways and lungs. Breathing is an automatic reflex function. As oxygen is used up the body collects carbon dioxide. It is this collection of carbon dioxide that sends a signal to the brain, which triggers the breathing process.

Breathing process
The ribs become raised, and the diaphragm depresses down. The lung sacs then expand and air is sucked in via the nose/mouth. Exhalation induces a reverse procedure: when the ribs return, the diaphragm relaxes, which in turn pushes the air out of the nose/mouth. During a snorkel dive the air in the lungs will compress, along with the total lung volume. When breathing compressed air at ambient pressure, the lung volume remains constant therefore each breath taken will contain the same total amount of air as a breath at the surface and at any depth we dive to.

Stomach (Gut)
The air within the stomach will behave by equalising automatically. However the diver should avoid drinking fizzy drinks before a dive to minimise the

effect of aerophagia (gas swallowing). This can lead to gastric rupture on ascent.

Dental Barotrauma is a condition suffered by divers with air cavities in dental fillings. It can be rectified by replacement of any offending fillings.

It is recommended that you tell your dentist that you are a diver.

Artificial Air Spaces
Mask Squeeze
The mask is the most common of the diver's artificial air-filled spaces. Air within the mask compresses on descent. If the diver fails to equalise the increasing pressure, they will notice the effects of increasing pressure as the mask presses on the face (mask squeeze). If not equalised this pressure may lead to burst blood vessels and possible blackout with disastrous results. To equalise the pressure the diver simply exhales gently through the nose into the mask.

Suit Squeeze
Dry suits are filled with air to compensate for the increasing pressure. As we descend the pressure will compress the dry suit and internal air. As well as resulting in a loss of buoyancy, the diver will be affected by the suit squeezing the body (suit squeeze). Suit squeeze can be avoided by allowing more air into the suit. Dry suits are an active part of diving which require special skills, which are introduced on a dry suit course.

As any gas volume will increase upon ascent it is important to remember any uncontrolled expanding air may lead to an increased rate of ascent, with possible lung damage, and 'decompression illness'. Buoyancy aids will be affected in a similar way as the dry suit. Although semi-drysuits are affected by changes in pressure, it is not possible to equalise the loss of buoyancy due to compression from increased water pressure

During recreational diving our bodies are affected by additional changes. These include:

Temperature
As the diver descends they will notice a change in temperature, as the water ultimately becomes colder. Even in tropical waters the diver will eventually notice a drop in body temperature. Body heat is conducted

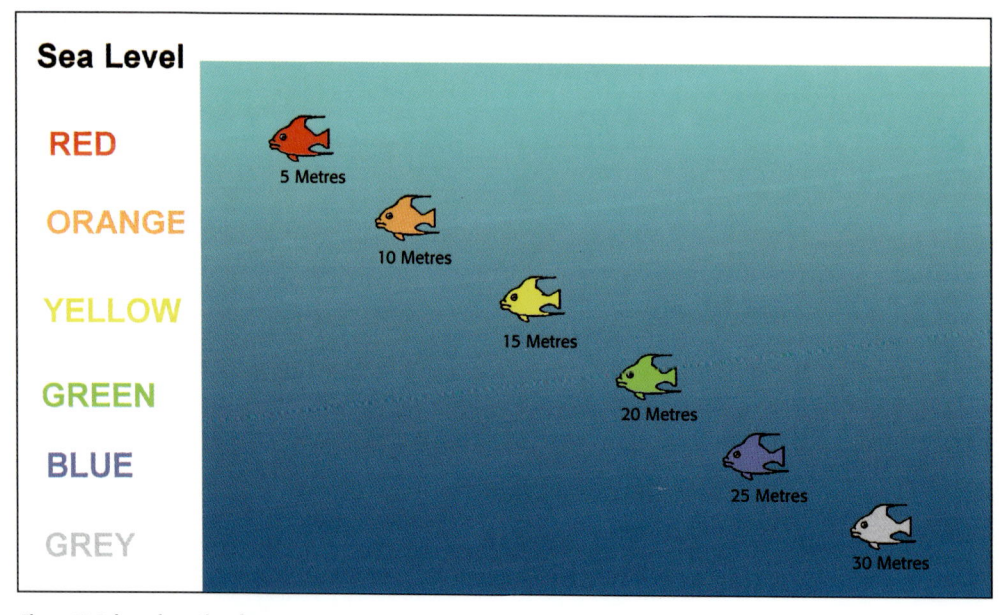

Sea Level

RED — 5 Metres
ORANGE — 10 Metres
YELLOW — 15 Metres
GREEN — 20 Metres
BLUE — 25 Metres
GREY — 30 Metres

Figure 67 Colour absorption changes

away from the body 25 times quicker in water than in air. In essence the deeper the diver goes the colder it will get. It is extremely important to avoid becoming hypothermic when diving.

Vision

Our vision is affected underwater. Objects, which are viewed underwater through a mask, will appear 33% larger and 25% closer; (marine life underwater is not really as big as it appears).

Light Absorption

The water absorbs light as depth increases. Daylight is made up of colours, which are absorbed at different depths. Red is the first colour to go, normally within the first few metres. Only blue light reaches great depths. Colour can be restored using artificial light such as a torch. However the drawback is that if there are a lot of suspended particles such as silt or plankton in the water, the torch light will simply be reflected back.

Sound

In air sound travels at approximately 350 metres per second, underwater this can increase to around 1500 metres per second. Sound travelling four times faster underwater can confuse the diver as to its direction and distance. The diver on the seabed will be able to hear an approaching ship from some distance. Sounds made above the water can seldom be heard below the water.

Chapter 6 Respiration, Circulation and Air Endurance

Metabolism

To survive and grow the body requires certain products to sustain life. Just as a car needs fuel to run its engine or a fire needs fuel to burn, the body needs energy to function effectively. The body is supplied with the nutrients it requires from the air around us and food we eat. This is known as 'Metabolism':

FOOD + OXYGEN = ENERGY + CARBON DIOXIDE

As a process metabolism produces:

ENERGY + CARBON DIOXIDE + WASTE PRODUCTS

Energy is required to move our bodies but this is used up in the process, whilst carbon dioxide is produced as a waste product of the respiratory system. Other waste by-products left over include sweat and bowel contents. The metabolic rate can differ from person to person: this means that some bodies take longer to use the available fuel and therefore produce less energy. In order to produce the power the energy has to pass through the body via the Respiration and Circulatory systems.

Respiration

Respiration is the process which transports oxygen (O^2) from the air that is inhaled and delivers it to the body tissues. As the tissues use the oxygen, carbon dioxide (CO^2) is produced and returned to the lungs so that it is released back into the atmosphere via exhalation. This process becomes clear when the composition of inhaled (breathing in) and exhaled air (breathing out) is examined.

Gas	Inhaled Air	Exhaled Air
Nitrogen, N^2	79 %	79 %
Other	1 %	1 %
Oxygen, O^2	20 %	16 %
Carbon dioxide, CO^2	Trace 4	%

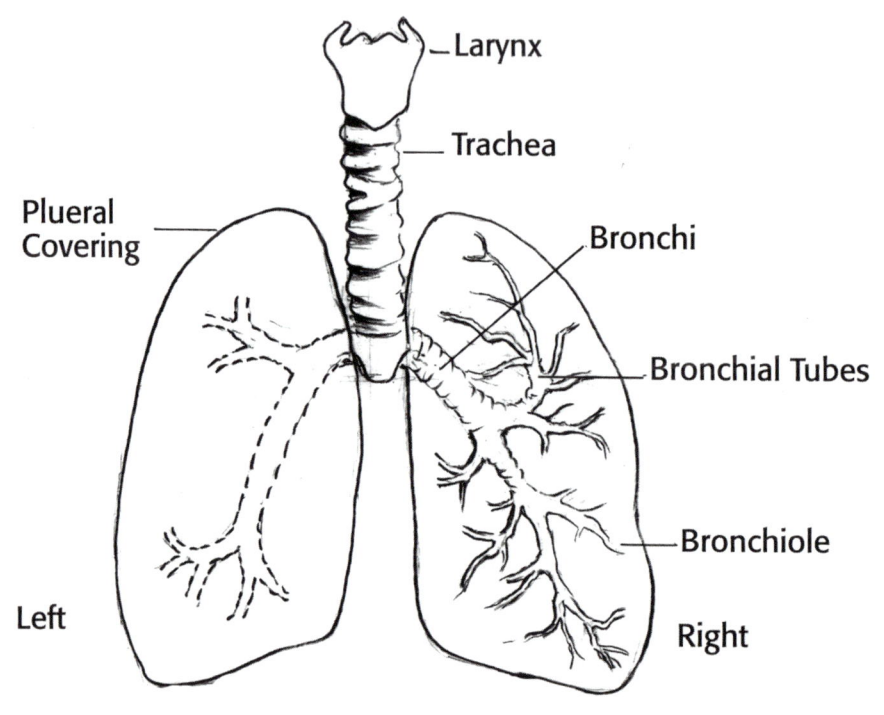

Figure 68 The lungs

It is apparent that whilst the air has been in the lungs, some of the oxygen has been used and a small amount of carbon dioxide added. Note that nitrogen is not involved in this process (i.e. it is non-metabolic), so that its contribution remains unaltered. Its importance is recognised for other reasons including nitrogen narcosis and decompression illness.

How is breathing accomplished?
Air is drawn into the lungs by the action of **intercostal muscles** and the **diaphragm**. To breathe in, the rib cage is pulled up as the diaphragm moves down. This increases the volume of the lungs, and allows air to move in to fill the space and increase the pressure in the lungs.

Breathing out is the reverse of this action. The lungs are 'squeezed' by letting the rib cage fall back into place allowing the diaphragm to return to its proper place. This results in the air being pushed out (exhaled).

Lungs
The lungs are the primary organs where the exchange of gases between the atmosphere and the blood actually takes place. They occupy, along with heart, almost the entire chest cavity. The lungs are rather dense organs, similar in structure to a sponge. Their function is to allow the transfer of oxygen and carbon dioxide between the air in the sac and the blood surrounding them, with oxygen moving from the air into the blood and carbon dioxide from the blood to the air. The lungs are completely filled with alveoli, providing a surface area approximately equal to the size of a tennis pitch.

The airways begin at the mouth and nose where air is drawn in. The **pharynx** (windpipe) passes air down into the throat, to the **larynx** (voice box), which is situated at the head of the **trachea**. This tube splits in two as it enters the chest, with these two pipes known as the **oesophagus** (gullet) and the **trachea**. In order to prevent any solids entering the trachea it is protected by a small flap known as the **epiglottis**. The **trachea** further splits in to two pipes known as bronchi, one for each lung. These in turn split into numerous smaller tubes called **bronchioles**. Each bronchiole splits many times and ends in a grape-like sac known as **alveoli**. There are around 600 million microscopic air sacs (**alveoli**) in the human body. It is in the alveoli that the actual interchange of gases takes place.

The lung sacs are coated in a slippery substance known as surfactant. This liquid helps stops the lungs from chafing against each other. Surface tension within the alveoli would add up to an enormous force, unless it was reduced by the existence of surfactant, which is a compound with similarities to soap.

Lung capacities
The lung capacity can be divided into various volumes. These are:
- **Total Lung Capacity**: This is maximum volume the lungs will hold when fully expanded (approximately 6.5 litres). Not all of this air is used in respiration.
- **Tidal Volume**: This is the amount of air that is used when at rest and is equal to about 0.5 litres.
- **Vital Capacity**: This is the term used to describe the amount of air that can be moved between maximum inspiration and maximum exhalation in one breath and accounts for 4.5 litres.
- **Residual Volume**: 1.5 litres is the amount of air that remains within the lungs after the maximum exhalation and represents the air which cannot be exhaled. This air is required to stop the lungs from collapsing.
- **Dead Air Space**: 0.5 litres is the amount of air that exists in the air space to the lungs.

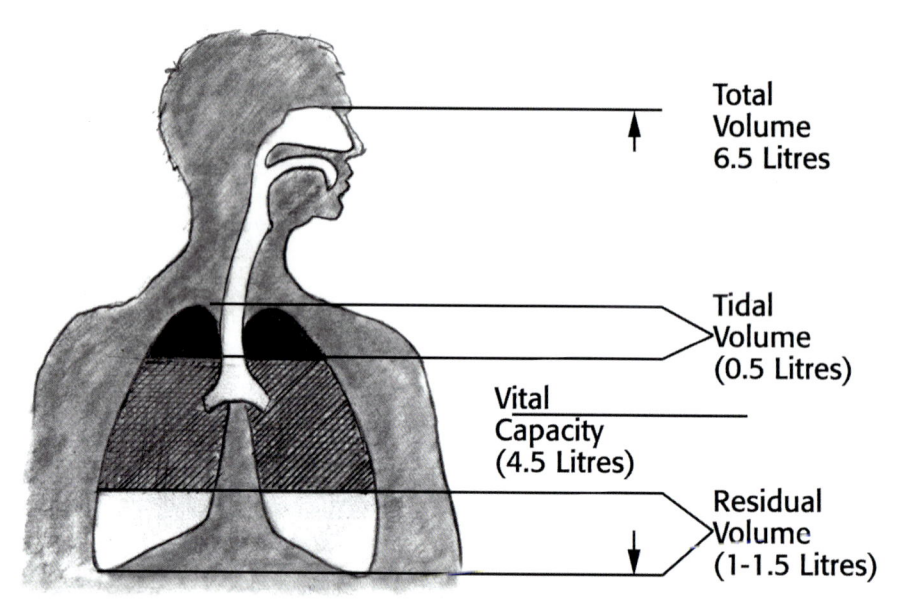

Figure 69 Lung capacities schematic

Air Consumption Table

Surface Breathing rate	Breathing rate at 10m	Breathing rate at 20m	Breathing rate at 30m	Breathing rate at 40m	Breathing rate at 50m
25 litres / min	50 litres / min	75 litres / min	100 litres / min	125 litres / min	150 litres / min

Circulatory System
Bloodstream
Oxygen is transported round the body in the blood. It is principally carried in red blood cells. The blood cells are shaped like discs to maximise their surface area, making the gaseous exchange easier. Red blood cells are full of a compound called **haemoglobin**, which has a strong affinity to oxygen. Oxygen can also be transported dissolved in blood plasma. The bloodstream is utilised for the transportation of carbon dioxide.

The Heart
The heart consists of many arteries and veins through which the blood supplies the organs with the blood (oxygen) that is required. The heart is the major body organ responsible for this task. The heart is divided into four chambers known as:

　　　　Right Ventricle　　　Left Ventricle
　　　　Right Atrium　　　　Left Atrium

The Atriums are the collecting chambers for blood returning to the heart. The Ventricles are the pumping chambers, which send the blood on its way. The two sides of the heart are made up of two different pressures. The right side being the low pressure side.

Heart/circulatory process
Blood is returned to heart via the **inferior vena cava** (the lower body) and the **superior vena cava** (the upper body). This blood is low in oxygen (venous blood) having supplied body tissues. The blood is collected in the **right atrium**

where it passes through a flap (tricuspid valve) into the **right ventricle**. The blood is then pumped out at low pressure to the lungs via the **pulmonary artery**. In the lungs the interchange of gases takes place through the **alveoli membrane**. Carbon dioxide is released in expired air and oxygen is taken in. This blood is then returned to the **left atrium** through the **pulmonary vein**. The blood passes through a flap (mitral valve) to the **left ventricle** where it is pumped out (arterial blood) at high pressure to the rest of the body via the **aorta**. The process starts all over again as the blood supplies the body with oxygen and takes up more carbon dioxide.

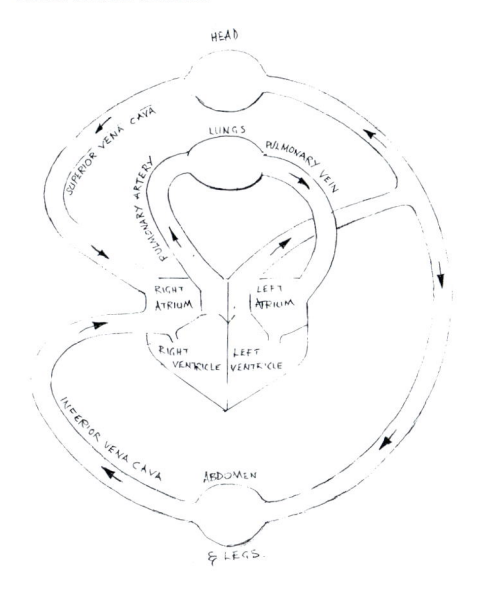

Figure 70 The circulatory system

The breathing rate (i.e. the number of breaths taken per minute) varies depending on the work rate. The harder the work rate, the more air is taken in, this occurs because energy is being burned faster requiring more oxygen.

Air consumption
An adult male may consume on average, around 6 litres of air in a minute, however with exercise this can easily double. The main factor in air consumption rates is likely to be the diver's depth. Other factors can affect how much air we use: these include the effort we are exerting, along with our mental and physical states. It is widely believed that personal diving experience is a contributing factor in air consumption. Divers with little experience suffer more from anxiety, thereby increasing air consumption rates.

Average air consumption, for a person at rest on the surface, is approximately 10 litres/minute. For an average person swimming on the surface, the rate may be considered to be around 25 litres/minute. It should be noted that all air endurance evaluation should be regarded as a rough guide only.

Unlike air, water is a very dense medium. Considering Boyle's Law is important in understanding how pressure rapidly increases air consumption as we descend and its effects.

The following simple equation can be used to interpret this: *Consumption rate at depth = Absolute pressure X Consumption rate at surface.* The table illustrates the difference depth has on our rate of air consumption.

Air Endurance
A diving cylinder has a fixed amount of air contained within it. This amount is dependent on the capacity of the cylinder and the pressure of the air within. Simple calculations enable the diver to work out his air endurance.

The maximum capacity of such a cylinder can be calculated using two of the cylinder specifications:

Water Capacity x Maximum Working Pressure = Total Air Capacity

For example, a 10-litre cylinder filled to its maximum working pressure of 232 Bar would contain 2320 litres, this is calculated as 10 litres x 232 bar

However, if the cylinder is not at its maximum working pressure (WP), perhaps due to having been used on a previous dive, then the air it contains will be determined using the following calculation:

> **Water Capacity x Gauge Pressure = Available Air**

If the contents gauge reads 100 bar, then the cylinder would contain 1000 litres of air. This is found calculating 10 litres x 100 bar. We can calculate the amount of air that is required for a particular dive using the following examples.

Example 1
A diver plans to dive to 25 metres. They have a 12-litre (WC) cylinder that has a working pressure (WP) of 232 bar. A reserve level of 50 bars has been decided upon. With air consumption rates based on a surface breathing rate of 25 litres/per minute. What dive duration can be expected?

Air available in cylinder	= WC x WP
	= 12 x 232
	= 2784 litres.
Chosen air reserve	= 12 x 50
	= 600 litres.
Air available for dive	= Cylinder air – Reserve air
	= 2784 – 600 = 2184 litres.
Breathing rate at depth	= rate at surface x absolute pressure at depth (25m = 3.5 bar)
	= 25 litres/minute x 3.5 bar
	= 87.5 litres/minute.
Dive duration	= Air available for dive divided by breathing rate at depth.
	= 2184 litres divided by 87.5 litres / minute
	= 25 minutes (approximately).

Example 2
A dive is planned to 30 metres (4 bar absolute), for 20 minutes.

Air consumption rate at surface	= 25 litres/minute
Breathing rate at depth	= 25 litres x 4 bar = 100 litres/minute.
Air required for dive	= Duration x Breathing rate at depth
	= 20 minutes x 100 litres/minute
	= 2000 litres.

A 10-litre cylinder with a working pressure of 232 bar would give enough air for the dive, however, the calculations above do not include any additional air for reserve air and would leave little room for any unforeseen circumstances. A better option would be to use a 12-litre cylinder with a working pressure of 232 bar. For precise calculations each part of the dive can be broken down into stages. It should be noted however that there are many variables in individual breathing rates which can affect actual air endurance limits.

Chapter 7 Diving Disorders and Decompression Illness

Burst Lung

Boyle's Law states that pressure varies inversely with volume, as the pressure increases the volume decreases, and vice versa.

As divers we breathe air at ambient pressure. At an absolute pressure of two bars (10m), twice the amount of air is required to fill the lungs to their normal capacity, as would be on the surface. For a diver who maintains normal lung volume during a dive, over expansion of the lungs on ascent (i.e. failure to exhale while ascending), poses a real danger. It can force air into the bloodstream or can cause lung tissue to rupture, trapping air in pockets in the chest cavity. The results of this can be dramatic. Injuries of this sort are collectively referred to as 'burst lung'.

Air Embolism

Tiny bubbles of air will enter the capillaries and thus the bloodstream if the alveolar membrane is allowed to overstretch. The circulation will carry these bubbles – which may unite into larger bubbles – to the brain, heart and other vital organs where they could lodge, blocking further blood flow (hence oxygen supply). Symptoms usually appear rapidly after surfacing and include giddiness, numbness, paralysis, visual disturbances, respiratory difficulties, heart failure and in extreme circumstance death.

Pneumothorax

In some cases the alveolar tissue may suffer a major tear, allowing air to escape outwards and become trapped between the lung sac and chest wall. If the ascent continues, the pressure of the

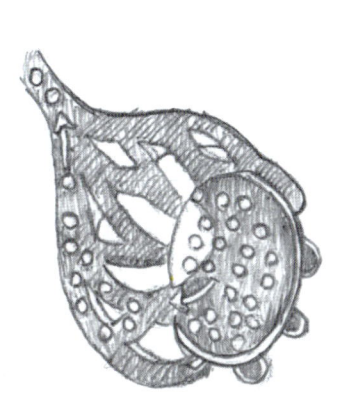

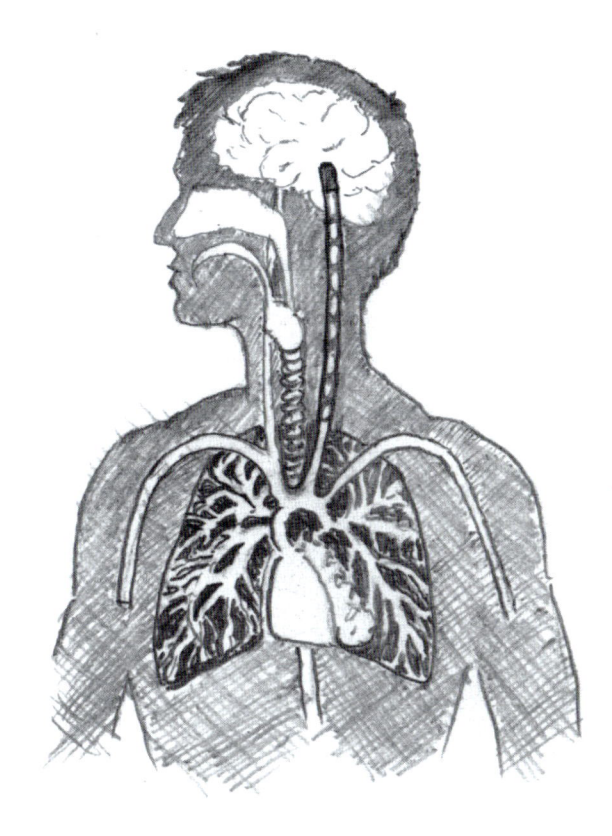

Figure 71 Air embolism

Figure 72 Spontaneous Pneumothorax

trapped air will be greater than that of the air in the lungs. This may cause the lung sacs to collapse. Symptoms include severe pain on breathing, shortness of breath, coughing of blood and swollen appearance of chest cage.

Interstitial Emphysema

Larger bubbles of air that escape from torn lung tissue can travel inwards between the lung sacs, into the vicinity of the heart and the major blood vessels. This trapped air will also have a serious effect on normal respiration. Symptoms include shortness of breath, swollen appearance of skin at base of neck and also those of air embolism.

In order to get to a point where the lung sac rips it will obviously have to have overstretched. For this reason symptoms of air embolism may also be present in both Pneumothorax and Emphysema. Burst lung conditions may also include effects and symptoms of hypoxia, since normal respiration is upset.

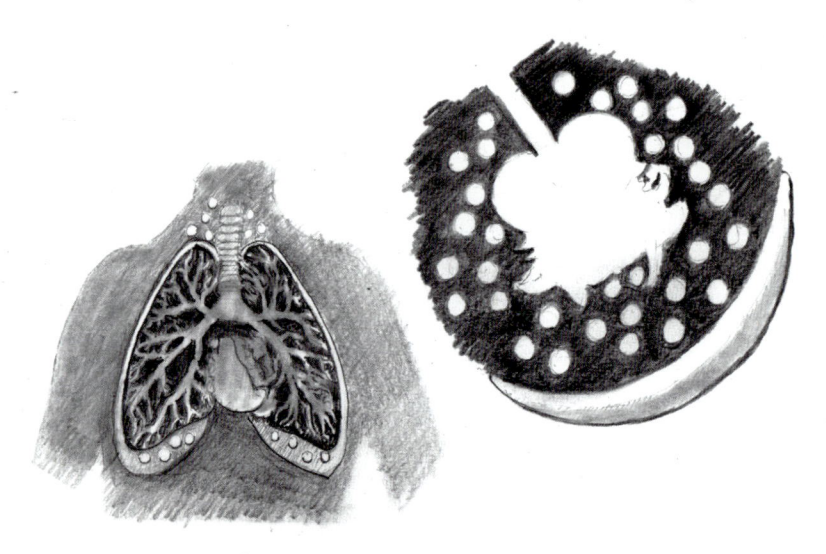

Figure 73 Interstitial Emphysema

Treatment

The only successful treatment for air embolism is immediate recompression in a chamber. Pneumothorax and emphysema may require surgical treatment. In all cases 100% oxygen should be administered immediately to the victim, consequently professional medical assistance should be sought immediately. Breathing should be closely monitored with the rescuer ready to administer artificial ventilation (AV) should it be necessary.

Some of the symptoms are the same for decompression illness and, although a correct diagnosis may be difficult at the scene, it makes little difference as the treatment is the same for both. In an effort to avoid the risks of burst lung divers should follow the golden rule of sub aqua diving.

ALWAYS BREATHE NORMALLY: NEVER HOLD YOUR BREATH ESPECIALLY DURING ANY ASCENT.

Decompression Illness (DCI)

The classification of 'decompression' is a reduction in ambient pressure as the diver ascends; this means any form of ascent can be referred to as 'decompression'. Decompression illness occurs primarily as a result of prolonged exposure to pressurised nitrogen. It was first noticed in 1877 when workmen doing heavy underground construction of a bridge were seen walking with a slight stoop. This gave rise to the term 'the bends'. It is reported that the terminology came about when persons afflicted with decompression illness gain some comfort from 'bending' the afflicted body organ (i.e. the arm or leg). Whichever reference is sought it is widely accepted that any reference to decompression illness is commonly known as a 'bend'.

In the 60s it was accepted that nitrogen leaves the body in a different manner to that in which it enters. It is a known fact that it is harder to get rid of absorbed nitrogen than it is to absorb it in the first place.

Confining dives to just one a day can assist in the prevention of decompression illness. Micro bubbles are often created by decompression, which in most cases have no harmful effect on the diver. However, when carrying out more than one dive per day (repetitive diving) so-called 'micro' bubbles can affect the diver by being washed by blood flow into the lungs. Once in the lungs the micro bubbles can restrict the release of residual nitrogen during the ascent. This would also apply to decompression stops and surface intervals (SI).

A further complication is that 'micro' bubbles from a previous dive may not be fully re-compressed during a subsequent dive thereby creating their own 'silent' bubbles. Over a number of dives the residual nitrogen build up may cause decompression illness even when staying within decompression tables.

Micro bubbles that accumulate in the lungs may persist for over three hours by which time the nitrogen bubbles will have dissolved from the system. In an effort to assist this off-gassing period the SAA recommends a minimum surface interval of three hours between subsequent dives.

The diver's body at the surface is saturated with nitrogen at atmospheric pressure, (1 bar). As the diver descends and spends time on a dive, the body will absorb more nitrogen into the tissues and blood. At 10 metres the body will absorb twice as much nitrogen.

During the ascent the reduction in ambient pressure will allow the nitrogen to come out of solution. As this happens bubbles may be formed. If an ascent is made too quickly the nitrogen will not be able to escape naturally through the lungs as we cannot exhale quickly enough. During a normal ascent small micro bubbles are formed but these will be released without consequence.

Boyle's Law taught us that all gases expand as we ascend.

These harmless bubbles can expand to cause severe problems. In the bloodstream the bubble may increase to a size that can block the flow of blood to tissues. Any restriction in blood flow will have the effect of starving the tissues and hence vital organs of the oxygen we need to survive.

The best example of this is a clear bottle of fizzy drink. We can see that, unopened, no bubbles are present. As the bottle is opened small bubbles are formed and rise to the surface. This is indicative of what happens to gas (nitrogen) within the bloodstream.

It is widely accepted that the rate of blood flowing through a tissue (perfusion) is of primary importance to the rate and speed with which a specific tissue will saturate with nitrogen. Tissues that are well perfused are known as fast tissues, these include the heart, brain, muscles or kidneys. It is these organs that will become quickly saturated.

If the diver were to ascend in an uncontrolled manner larger bubbles might form with serious consequences. Going back to our bottle of fizzy drink, if it is shaken before opening, the gas will form many bubbles and froth as it is opened. This is what would happen to the nitrogen in the diver's bloodstream. Factors which can contribute to decompression illness include: cold, dehydration, obesity, age, exertion/exhaustion, effects of alcohol, and some physical injuries. The reason for this is thought to be the change in tissue perfusion.

The probability of decompression illness can also be influenced by: repetitive diving, deep diving, very long shallow dives, flying (or ascending to a higher altitude after diving), carbon dioxide level, Patent Foraman Ovale (PFO) presence, anxiety, drug use and dehydration. The likelihood of its occurrence is increased by repeated exposure to depth.

Tissues with a poor blood supply such as joints, cartilages or tendons are referred to as slow tissues. It should be noted that whilst fat does not have a high perfusion rate it does however, have a high affinity to nitrogen and absorbs it at an increased rate.

A diver's susceptibility to DCI can change from day to day. Some dives do not allow enough gas to escape during the ascent, and the diver is required to carry out a decompression stop (stage stop) on the way up. This is known as decompression diving and should be attempted by experienced divers only.

Decompression Illness can be divided into two types:

Mild Decompression Illness
- Mild symptoms include pain around the joints, skin rashes and itching.
- The pain is most common around joints, particularly the knees and shoulders
- There can be a mild pain for a few hours or a severe pain lasting over 12 hours, increasing in severity.
- Skin rashes and itching whilst less severe are equally important. They should be regarded as a warning sign.

Severe Decompression Illness
Symptoms can be wide ranging and may include:
- Numbness, tingling, weakness, paralysis, vision problems, balance disturbances, confusion and convulsions.
- Within the heart and lungs considerable amounts of bubbles can be formed into a froth that interferes with the circulation of blood. This would generally appear shortly after surfacing and if not treated promptly can be fatal.
- In extreme circumstances some bubbles can pass through to the arterial blood system. This is an extremely serious condition, which can affect the blood (oxygen) supply to the body's tissues and brain.

Damage to the Central Nervous System (CNS) is more serious as in many cases the damage caused is irreparable and can be fatal.

Treatment

The only treatment for DCI is recompression. This involves specialist equipment manned by highly trained operators. The casualty is recompressed to a pressure usually equivalent to 18m of sea water, The casualty breathes pure oxygen for much of the process to flush out as much Nitrogen from their system as possible. The high Pp of oxygen is beneficial to any tissue suffering a reduced blood flow as a result of the DCI. The casualty is brought back to surface pressure at a very carefully determined rate, and will be thoroughly examined by a Hyperbaric physician for any signs of damage to their nervous system.

This treatment can only be carried out in a specially equipped medical centre with a recompression chamber and staffed by qualified personnel. **Under NO CIRCUMSTANCES should recompression be attempted by a diver re-entering the water.**

On site the diver should be given oxygen as soon as possible. This will raise the level of oxygen to hypoxic tissues and help reduce the level of nitrogen. It will also help flush excess nitrogen out of the system. It should not be used as a replacement for recompression. The casualty should be laid down and kept still and warm. It would be a wise precaution to monitor the buddy as they have probably followed the same dive profile and may suffer similar symptoms.

Divers suffering from Decompression Illness should NEVER be given ENTONOX, which is carried by ambulances for pain relief. Entonox contains nitrous dioxide, which may increase any bubbles, making problems worse.

These first aid measures in no way replace the expert treatment of decompression illness by recompression. Symptoms of decompression illness do not always show themselves immediately. They are likely to be present in 50% of cases within 1/2 hour of surfacing, with most cases occurring within six hours. However, in some cases symptoms may not develop until more than 24 hours after the dive terminated.

In terms of first aid at the diving site, it is essential that the authorities are alerted as soon as possible. This involves contacting the coastguard, either by VHF radio on channel 16, or by dialling 999. The coastguard will ask for details of the symptoms as well as precise aspects relating to the dives performed. The strategic accident management will then be in the hands of the specialists.

Hypoxia

As we described earlier, the body requires oxygen to survive. Too much oxygen can be toxic, but if the body has a shortage of oxygen it can be equally life threatening. The brain cells will start to die if starved of oxygen for more than 3 minutes, whilst muscle cells can survive for around 30 minutes.

Hypoxia is determined as 'lack of oxygen'. Contributing factors to hypoxia include:
- An obstruction of the airway
- Damaged or diseased lung(s) e.g. a burst lung
- Carbon monoxide poisoning
- When the heart is unable to pump with sufficient force to supply all the body tissues
- An extraordinary incident such as hyperventilation or drowning
- A reduced amount of oxygen in the gas being breathed
- A faulty diving regulator, restricting the flow of air
- Lack of breathable air (as in drowning)

The diver who is hypoxic may exhibit signs such as:
- Drowsiness
- Lack of co-ordination
- Headache

- Increased respiration and pulse rate
- Lips/nails/ear lobes turning blue (cyanosis)
- Cyanosis (blueness of ear lobes, finger ends) and breathlessness, due to the raised partial pressure of carbon dioxide.
- Unconsciousness and death

Drowning and hypoxia are related conditions. It is essential to avoid becoming hypoxic. For aqualung divers this means ensuring that equipment is functioning adequately, that the cylinder is filled with the correct gas mixture for the planned dive, and that there is sufficient air to complete the dive and any stops that may be required. If an aqualung diver maintains a normal respiration rate he is unlikely to suffer from hypoxia. Each time we breathe the body is supplied with fresh oxygen.

As a diver becomes hypoxic the body's tissues will be starved of the vital oxygen they need. The casualty will suffer from cyanosis: The earlobes, nail beds, and lips will appear blue. This will be difficult to diagnose in a fully kitted diver who may also be suffering from the cold. At this stage lack of oxygen to the brain will cause the diver to develop poor co-ordination and he will become fatigued.

If a hypoxic diver is not treated they may well suffer convulsions and ultimately become unconscious. If this happens underwater it may result in death.

Treatment
The treatment for hypoxia is to restore natural breathing and the correct supply of air. Once the diver/casualty is back on the surface they should be given 100% oxygen to supply tissues which may be starved of oxygen. If oxygen is not available the diver could breathe from a nitrox cylinder, which has an enriched oxygen mixture. There would be no benefit in breathing compressed air from a dive cylinder as this contains only the same amount of oxygen as the surrounding air. Divers breathing normal compressed air at reasonable depths are not likely to suffer from hypoxia if the levels of oxygen are kept to a safe limit.

Drowning
The cause of drowning is typically the inhalation of fluids to the lungs. Drowning can cause death if water is allowed to enter the lungs and interfere with the transport of oxygen.

Drowning prevents oxygen from reaching the body tissues, i.e. it causes hypoxia. The term drowning should only be applied if death occurs. Individuals who inhale water but are resuscitated have experienced a *'near drowning'* situation. One of the most common causes of a diver drowning is when the diver runs out of air. Every diver should be equipped with a contents gauge, although it will be useless if it is not monitored effectively.

The initial reaction from the body when water is inhaled is to have a laryngeal spasm causing a cough, just as when food goes down the wrong way. This may have disastrous consequences if it happens underwater. The casualty would become hypoxic followed by unconsciousness and eventually by death. If water is allowed to enter the airway the oesophagus will stop it entering the lungs and divert it to the stomach. This is known as "dry drowning".

In most cases where death has occurred the victim has water in their lungs. As the diver become unconscious the oesophagus will relax allowing water to enter the lungs drowning the victim. This is more commonly referred to as "wet drowning".

Symptoms
- Coughing
- Shortness of breath
- Chest pain
- Shock
- Cyanosis (blue lips and finger nail beds)
- Unconsciousness
- Irregular breathing or no breathing
- Weak or absent pulse

Treatment

Remove the casualty from the water and begin AV/CPR (artificial ventilation/cardio pulmonary resuscitation) immediately if required. 100% oxygen should be administered if possible. The casualty may suffer from shock and hypothermia and should be monitored at all times until professional help arrives.

If the casualty improves they must still be taken to hospital as there is a high risk of 'secondary drowning] seventy-two hours after the event. The water inhaled into the lungs can damage the alveolar membrane. These react by excluding the water slowly from within the blood. This fluid will eventually fill the lungs (secondary drowning).

Hyperventilation

Snorkel divers use hyperventilation to increase the length of time they can stay down. It can be accomplished by taking a series of very deep breaths prior to breath holding and commencing the dive. This will have the effect of reducing the levels of carbon dioxide (the gas which gives us the desire to breathe). However, the drawback with this is that hyperventilation does not correspondingly increase the levels of oxygen. The lowering of carbon dioxide in the body is called hypocapnia. Secondary receptors in the heart and brain detect the lack of oxygen (O^2), before the carbon dioxide (CO^2) trigger is reached. The diver will be in danger of becoming unconscious. The best form of treatment is avoidance. This means that divers should breathe normally throughout the dive.

Take only 2 medium deep breaths, at most, before setting off on a breath-holding dive. Never overwork or linger at depth.

Hypercapnia

Hypercapnia (too much carbon dioxide) can be just as much of a problem. It will make the diver breathless, and he will most likely suffer a throbbing headache, followed by dizziness and confusion. Hypercapnia is most common when using full-face masks, skipping a breath, or using faulty regulators, where the diver has to work hard to breathe. The problem is exacerbated by depth.

Exhaustion

Exhaustion can be typically defined as 'being unable to meet the demands (physically and/or mentally) that the body requires'. The diver who becomes exhausted may leave himself at a higher risk of decompression illness. A diver's rate of air consumption may also increase as they become tired/exhausted. If this happens during a dive the diver should take hold of a stationary object to recover and then if necessary abandon the dive.

It would be foolish to carry on. Carrying on may put both yourself and your buddy in a life-threatening situation. Something may happen that you are unable to cope with. The dive should be one within your capabilities.

The diver can quite easily demand more from the demand valve that it can give. This is known as 'beating the lung'. Exhaustion is a condition that is more easily recognised than defined. Divers should be able to recognise the signs and symptoms as well as knowing how to deal with them. Late nights and early starts feature heavily in exhaustion equations.

Deep diving and stage diving makes a diver more susceptible to exhaustion. As depth increases, so does air density and consequently breathing resistance. At 30m, the diver's maximum ventilation rate is halved and the ability to eliminate carbon dioxide becomes diminished. At depth, it becomes increasingly important to avoid heavy exertion in any form. Such behaviour is not only wasteful of air, it can also lead to an increased likelihood of nitrogen narcosis and decompression illness.

Hardworking muscles undertaking strenuous lifting/finning may become overloaded. This will induce the production of excess lactic acid.

Lactic acid will create a dull ache in the muscles and increases the blood's acidity. This stimulates the breathing reflex in the same way as carbon dioxide. Laboured breathing will continue after the exertion has ceased, allowing the body to reclaim the oxygen debt built up by the exertion. It is important that the sequence of activities which contributed to the initial exhaustion is not repeated.

Treatment
Minimise exertion whilst diving. The effects of tide, current and surface wind/swell should be taken into account. This will not only avoid the diver's becoming exhausted, but is essentially good diving technique.
- Do not dive if feeling tired, cold or unwell.
- Signal to dive buddy as soon as the effects of exertion are suspected.

When the surface is reached, the condition of the exhausted diver should be monitored. Buoyancy compensators should be fully inflated. If conditions permit, the mask and demand valve should be removed. Appropriate signals, depending on the severity of the situation, should be given to the shore/boat cover. After regaining the shore/boat, rest and warm drinks should be administered and the individual's condition should be monitored as shock can follow exhaustion.

Hypothermia
Even in the warmest waters it is possible to suffer from hypothermia (excessive cooling). The normal body core temperature is 37°C; a drop in core temperature of just 2 degrees may cause shivering and discomfort which signal the first stages of hypothermia.

Water is an excellent conductor of heat (25 times more than air), and will take heat from the body, rapidly cooling it down. Heat loss is related to the surface area of the body and the rate of heat production is related to body volume. Therefore, smaller individuals such as children are more susceptible to hypothermia because their surface area to body volume ratio is small.

Hypothermia/loss of body heat results not only in physical discomfort but also in slow mental reactions and loss of muscle power and may lead to exhaustion contributing to many accidents. To continue with a dive whilst feeling chilled is not only foolhardy but also dangerous. The diver can become hypothermic by simply travelling in a boat to or from a dive, as a result of the wind chill effect. Any dive should be aborted if the diver is feeling cold. By the time shivering sets in significant body cooling has started.

A wind speed of 10 miles per hour will have a temperature reducing effect of around - 14°C. This would rapidly bring the body temperature down below the safe tolerance level.

The extremities (hands, feet etc.) are less dependent on temperature and can withstand lower temperatures. Reduced blood flow to the extremities will result in less heat being lost in the body core. The body will sense this and attempts to reduce the blood level by passing more water through the kidneys i.e. urine production is increased. Core temperature is crucial and a fall of only 1-2 degrees will prompt hypothermia.

Signs & Symptoms
35°C - 36°C	Sensation of cold, numbness, 'goose pimples', controllable and then uncontrollable shivering occurs. Metabolic and respiratory rate increases.
34°C - 35°C	Heart, metabolic and respiratory rates begin to decrease, causing confusion, lethargy and behavioural changes.
33°C	Amnesia begins, shivering stops and muscles become rigid. Mental confusion and communication difficulties. Semi-consciousness occurs.

30°C	Unconsciousness
28°C	Respiration becomes erratic
25°C	Death

It should be stressed that there are considerable individual differences in the experience of and variability in reactions of different people to cold. Factors such as weight, fitness levels and overall health will affect the susceptibility to hypothermia.

Treatment
Remove from cold and protect from wind chill. The casualty should change into warm clothing (where possible). They should be gently re-warmed by warm drinks and/or the use of an exposure blanket.

Serious hypothermia can be a life-threatening situation and professional medical assistance should be sought immediately. Handling of the casualty should be kept to a minimum, avoid local heat and do not rub extremities. The casualty should lie still with their feet raised, this will help to contain the blood within the body's core and help prevent shock, caused by any fall in blood pressure.

Giving alcohol causes blood vessels to dilate and permits cold peripheral blood to return to the body's core. Cold blood may rush into the torso and cause a further drop in the core temperature (*afterdrop*), this is a major factor in 're-warming' deaths.

Hyperthermia
Hyperthermia, otherwise known as over-heating is less common than hypothermia because open water is naturally cooler than the body temperature. The diver is at risk of hyperthermia when suited up on a hot day out of the water. The body temperature will rise as it would do if suffering from a fever.

Signs & Symptoms
- Rapid breathing
- Feeling warm/hot
- Mental confusion
- Fatigue
- Muscle cramps
- Nausea
- Exhaustion

It goes without saying that the higher the temperature the worse the problem. Treatment for hyperthermia is to cool the body. This can be done by covering the body in a wet blanket, immersing the body in water, or spraying/soaking the body with water. Cooling the body temperature should be done at a steady pace. It is possible that the diver could go into shock or suffer from hypothermia if the temperature is reduced too quickly.

Chapter 8 Accident Avoidance and Rescue Procedures

The following information should be used as a guide only. The circumstances required to successfully perform the rescue can be varied and wide. What may be suitable for one type of rescue may be inappropriate for another. There are no set rules by which a rescue should be performed. Your way of performing a rescue may be different to someone else. A rescuer should only attempt their best. The overriding point is that whatever the rescuer does they must not put themselves in a position of danger.

Accidents are a culmination of events and are rarely caused by one single action. It can be as simple as continuing a dive when the diver is cold or exhausted. As events unfold the diver may be unable to cope: it is at this point that stress and panic might set in.

The following can be a good guide to signs of stress/impending panic:
- Nervousness
- Irregular breathing
- Orientation changes
- Problems with a small dilemma
- No response to given signals
- Wide staring eyes
- Eagerness to surface/constantly facing to the surface

Whilst it is not really possible to fully train for all the circumstances that the diver may come across there are some additional considerations that can help avoid an incident.

Figure 74 Pool practice in rescue tow techniques

Emergency training

Basic emergency training is given during diver instruction with further preparation available as an extra course. Training focuses on trying to prepare for unexpected eventualities. It is not known when or indeed if these skills will be put to the test. The oxygen administration course teaches divers the necessary skills for administering oxygen to a diver as well as introducing oxygen equipment. Oxygen (O_2) should only be administered to divers and not to the general public.

Certification is awarded to successful candidates, whilst the first aid course looks at the techniques of general diver first aid.

Diver's skills and knowledge in particular areas

It is easy for a diver to submit to 'peer' pressure and push themselves beyond their limitations and abilities. Accidents have occurred when divers have dived beyond their training, some with disastrous results. Having the correct skills and knowledge will assist the diver. It is accepted that stress can exacerbate problems. If possible the diver should aim to be relaxed in their environment. Rescue situations can be a traumatic experience for everyone.

Personal equipment

The diver is dependent on their equipment and should strive to be familiar with its use and limitations. It is inadvisable to use new equipment for the first time in open water. The best solution is for the diver to first try any major changes to their equipment in a sheltered environment. You may be faced with using your buddy's equipment in a rescue situation so should endeavour to be acquainted with it.

Regular training

It is advisable that emergency skills be regularly practised in order to be of use. Rescue skills can become stale if it has been some time since the skills were originally learnt. Regular practice ensures that divers' emergency skills are proficient.

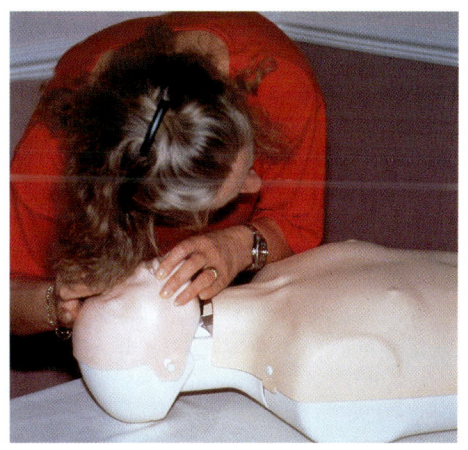

Figure 75 First aid resuscitation training

Fitness

Before a diver undergoes any form of training they are expected to complete a medical, or have filled in a UK Sport Diver Medical Form (self declaration yearly). Clubs can insist on normal medicals by GPs. One of the things that are hard to confirm is a diver's personal fitness level. Diving is a sport that requires a reasonable standard of fitness. The level of fitness can change from time to time especially during any protracted lay off such as the winter period.

Alcohol

Alcohol should be taken sparsely; diving and alcohol don't mix very well. Any diver drinking before a dive is putting both himself and his buddy at great risk. Alcohol and underwater pressure can reduce a diver's capacity to deal with an incident. Mental ability will be reduced: this may mean an inability to recognise what is happening in his surroundings. Alcohol stays in the body for some time, so excessive alcohol the evening before a dive should be avoided as the level of alcohol in the blood system may still affect the diver the following day. Alcohol can also increase the effects of seasickness, and increase chances of decompression illness (bends).

Drugs

Many of the problems associated with alcohol apply to the diver taking medication. Many of the medications that can be purchased from a chemist without the need for a doctor's prescription are unsuitable for diving. Anyone undergoing a course of medication should consult their doctor to check its suitability. Any drug labelled as one which may cause any form of drowsiness, should be avoided. One of the dangers of using medications to clear sinuses or seasickness is that they may wear off prematurely.

Dive planning

Good dive planning is essential to ensure that dives are carried out adequately. Dive planning ensures that emergency procedures are in place. Competent dive planning will take into account any possible problems and the actions that may be required to overcome them. This can be just ensuring that each diver has the air available for the planned dive. This planning should include making sure adequate first aid measures are considered. This should include having a good first aid kit and an oxygen set available at all times.

Rescue management

Contemplating making a rescue can be broken down into four stages;

- Stop
- Assess
- Plan
- Act

Stop

Stop whatever else you are doing until you have dealt with the emergency

Assess

Assessing the situation should ensure that nobody is put at risk. This is the divers opportunity to choose what resources are available for completing the task safely. A short time assessing the situation can save valuable time later. This is your opportunity to take charge if you feel you can do so. Give instructions to those who can help.

Plan

Once you have assessed the situation, you can now plan the necessary actions. The assessment will have given aims and priorities that must be addressed. Other people may have observed something that you have missed. Any plan should be explained and understood by everyone.

Act

Having assessed and planned the situation it is now time to act. The leader must allocate the necessary tasks to those who can carry them out proficiently. It is best to allocate those tasks to people that are suitably trained. A simple example of this is to allocate any first aid to a qualified first aider. Whilst a qualified boatman can be given control of the boat duties. Any serious situation should be reported to the coastguard, using a VHF radio on channel 16. If required they will organise any helicopter evacuation.

Record

It is important to record the incident and any events / actions, the dive profile may be required by the coastguard in order to advise a recompression chamber. The records should be sent with the casualty. The casualty's computer should also go with them if they have one. Many chambers can download the information to get a precise picture of the dive profile undertaken by the diver.

If decompression illness is suspected in any incident the buddy should also be monitored, as there is a risk they may suffer similar effects. Remember decompression illness may not always be immediately apparent. The buddy should not be involved in the rescue process, it is best that they are given reassurance therefore someone should be allocated the task of looking after them.

Any diving equipment that was used in any incident should not be tampered with. If necessary it may be collected by the police so that it can be analysed and tested.

Re-assess
Throughout any incident you will need to continually assess the situation. It may be that things require changing to meet the requirements. Always be ready to modify any plans where necessary.

Stress
There will also be the relatives to consider. It is essential to make sure that important facts are not disclosed to the press. These could be misconstrued causing further distress to the casualty, to those involved, or the relatives. In any accident those involved may suffer from stress after the incident has been dealt with. Do not be afraid to seek help where required.

Diver assistance
Diver assistance can be as simple as towing a tired diver, or just helping carry equipment. The first step in assisting a diver is to encourage them to help themselves. In open water instruct the diver to inflate their buoyancy compensator. Reassure them that you can help them. If they are unable to do it themselves you may have to do it for them. The decision to tow a tired diver is best left as the last option unless you know that other help cannot be reached easily. Towing a diver can be extremely physically demanding. If faced with towing the diver some distance then you may have to dump the casualty's equipment (weightbelt/cylinder) to make the tow easier.

Before approaching any casualty, extreme caution should be taken. Approaching a panicking casualty may lead to disastrous consequences. If they are in a state of panic they may try to climb up you to get out of the water, pushing you down. If left alone the casualty will soon calm down, the rescuer can then approach him safely. The casualty should always be approached from behind. You should be ready to take evading action if necessary. The simplest way of doing this is to submerge: this is the last place the casualty wants to be.

Rescue techniques
Emergency ascents
It is possible that throughout our diving career we may never have to make an emergency ascent, however divers should have an understanding of what to do in an emergency. Good training and experience is essential in dealing with an emergency situation. The diver rescue course is an ideal way of increasing the personal rescue skills that one day may stand you in good stead. It is worth noting that if faced with any sort of emergency the diver making the rescue must go with the decision they feel is right for the occasion.

Making any emergency ascent carries a greater risk of decompression illness and possible pressure damage. The most common reason for making an emergency ascent is running out of air. This is generally because divers fail to monitor their gauges effectively and not because of regulator malfunctions. The preferred choice of emergency ascent is a buddy assisted ascent. This can be done utilising the alternative air source carried by the buddy (the octopus) or by sharing a single regulator (buddy breathing). For either of these to work it is essential that both divers are within easy reach of each other.

Using an alternative air source is the easiest and safest way of making an emergency ascent. The diver would approach his buddy giving the 'out-of-air' signal. Both divers should approach each other. The assisting diver should offer the alternative air source (octopus) to the diver at eye level. The diver would not know they were out of air until they attempted to breathe in, therefore they may not have enough air in their lungs to clear any water from the demand valve. It is essential that the purge button is left unrestricted.

Because the diver may run out of air unknown to his buddy it is important to make sure the octopus is easily accessible. There is little point in tucking it safely inside a buoyancy compensator pocket.

Buddy breathing ascent

The buddy breathing emergency ascent is fraught with problems if the skill is unpractised. This skill must be mastered in the safe confines of the pool before trying in open water. Practise a dry run on the surface showing what holds and positions are suitable.

A diver out of air should give the appropriate signal. Both divers then approach each other, with the assisting diver offering his demand valve to his buddy after taking a deep breath. Both divers should remain static until a comfortable rhythm is established. Each diver would take two breaths before releasing it for the other diver to take a breath. The donor of the demand valve should always retain a firm grip of his valve. When passing the demand valve to the buddy it should be passed at eye level with the purge button unrestricted.

If divers find themselves without air and their buddy is not in sight, they will have no option but to ascend to the surface. To make it easier to swim to the surface the diver may dump their weightbelt to gain positive buoyancy. Because any residual air will expand on ascent the diver should be aware that the rate of ascent would also increase. The diver should flare his fins to create additional drag, especially in the final few metres.

The biggest danger is fear and a compelling desire to reach the surface. It is important to slow the ascent during the final few metres. When making the ascent it is essential that the diver continually exhales gently. In the final stages they should breathe out faster as the air expands. No ascent should be made using an octopus or when buddy breathing until both divers are ready. Both divers will still have to control the rate of ascent.

Diver rescue

Entry-level courses do not include complete diver rescue, however divers are introduced to the basics. This training will help prepare the diver with the basic skills necessary for diver rescue should they be required. Each incident is different and thus different techniques apply. There are many considerations involved in making a rescue: what one diver may do may be different to what another diver might do.

The first thing the rescuer should ask themselves is whether a rescue or simple assistance is required. It could be assisting to adjust a piece of equipment or supplying an alternative air source if needed.

The three basic objectives of any rescue are;
- To preserve life
- To prevent the condition from worsening
- To promote recovery

Recovering the casualty from depth

The priority is to get the casualty to the surface. In order to do this the recommended method is to use a 'Buoyant lift'. This is the safest method and the best method the rescuer has of controlling things.

Buoyant lift

The most important factor when carrying out any rescue is to ensure you have a secure grip of the casualty. The position of the rescuer and casualty should allow face-to-face contact and allow access to buoyancy controls. A side-frontal position is often found to be the best position. It is recommended that you experiment with different holds on different buddies.

A buoyant lift is made using the buoyancy provided by the casualty's suit or buoyancy compensator. This ensures that if separation occurs the casualty will still arrive at the surface. The added positive buoyancy will bring the diver up at a rate that exceeds normal ascent rates. This type of emergency carries the greatest risk from pressure injuries and decompression illness.

To initiate a buoyant lift the rescuer would add air to the buoyancy compensator (BC). The rescuer should be aware that the casualty would most likely have been using the dry suit for routine buoyancy. This air would expand on ascent and would require venting along with the air added to the BC during the emergency ascent. They should control the ascent rate as best they can under the circumstances.

Any symptoms of air embolism will generally be obvious immediately upon surfacing, however, the diver should be carefully monitored for signs of decompression illness, which may not be symptomatic straight away. During training courses divers are taught many important skills, however because of the increased risks of burst lung, 'free' and 'buoyant' ascents are not normally practised. The use of an alternative air source such as an octopus is the recommended method of making an emergency ascent. Buddy breathing should still be practised as a back-up method.

Although making any ascent is stressful it is important to remember that you must breathe out during the ascent. Whilst the other diver is breathing from the regulator the other diver should gently breathe out through their mouth as they were shown during their initial pool training.

Basic First Aid

Whilst not always life threatening the diver may be faced with a situation calling for some basic first aid care. Every diver should aim to have a basic understanding of treating minor injuries, as left unattended a minor injury could become life threatening.

Choking

Choking occurs when something becomes lodged in the back of the throat, blocking the windpipe. A choking casualty may exhibit difficulty breathing. Encourage the casualty to try and cough out the obstruction.

If further assistance is required there are two methods of help. Standing to the side of the casualty lean him forward so that when the foreign object is dislodged it falls out of the mouth. Give up to 5 sharp blows to the back between the shoulder blades.

If this does not work it will be necessary to use 'abdominal thrusts'. Stand behind the casualty and place both arms around the upper part of the abdomen just below the rib cage. Clenching your fist grab it with your other hand, then pull sharply inwards and upwards. The sudden movements force air out of the lungs in an attempt to dislodge the obstruction. Give up to 5 thrusts then more back blows if necessary.

Bleeding

When blood is lost from the circulation system, vital body organs can become starved of oxygen. Immediate action is necessary to stop the blood loss before shock sets in. The sight of blood is alarming to many individuals regardless of how much is lost. You should try to stay calm. If possible the best course of action is to apply pressure to the wound with a sterile dressing, and elevate the wounded limb where possible.

In the event that there are no sterile dressings available, it will be necessary to improvise with something clean. Reassure the casualty;

encourage them to remain still, as this will help the formation of clotting. This will help to stop the bleeding and assist in preventing infection. In cases where there is a foreign body embedded in an open wound, then it is best to place a dressing over the object where possible or to the side to avoid pushing it further in. It is best left in place as this may effectively be blocking a major tear.

Major Bleeding

If the blood loss is severe, direct pressure on the wound alone may not be sufficient. It may be necessary to apply pressure to one of the main arteries/pressure points close to the affected part of the body.

Shock

Shock is often present in most casualties. An individual suffering from shock will have skin that is pale and cool. Respiration may be shallow and rapid, with a rapid and weak pulse. They may be sweating profusely and have an intense thirst. They are likely to appear confused and anxious. The casualty may be nauseous, possibly faint.

To treat a person suffering from shock, they should be laid down flat. The reason for the shock should be attended to e.g. stop further bleeding. Administering 100% oxygen will restore the imbalance of oxygen-starved tissues. Fluids should be avoided. Reassure the casualty and monitor breathing. Shock is often overlooked and can lead to circulatory collapse and death in extreme circumstances.

Emergency Life Support

To survive the brain must be adequately supplied with oxygen. To facilitate this three things are required:

- **A**irway open and unobstructed to allow air to pass to the lungs.
- **B**reathing, delivering the air into the lungs where oxygen can then enter the bloodstream.
- **C**irculation must be sufficient to carry the blood carrying the oxygen from the lungs to the body tissues.

Resuscitation is the term used for the emergency treatment should one or more of the above fail. Approach the casualty with care, making sure it is safe to do so. Your first action should be assess whether the casualty is unconscious. Speak loudly to the victim. Enquire 'What has happened?' or 'Areyou alright?'. There will be no response from the unconscious victim.

Artificial Ventilation (AV)

It is essential to ascertain whether the casualty is breathing or requires assistance. Start by tilting the head and lift the chin. In an unconscious victim there is a danger of the tongue blocking the airway: tilting the head back and lifting the chin forward will draw the tongue from the back of the throat.

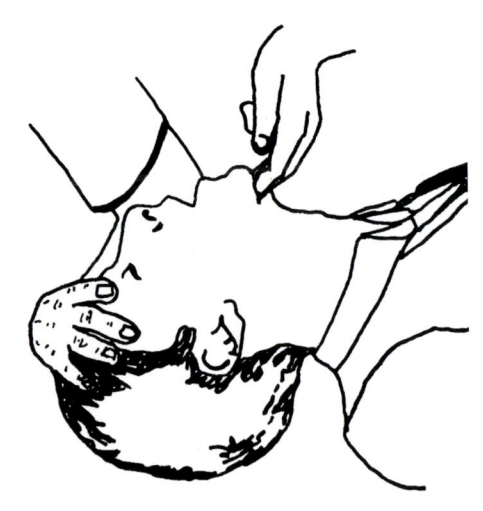

Figure 76 Raise the head and chin

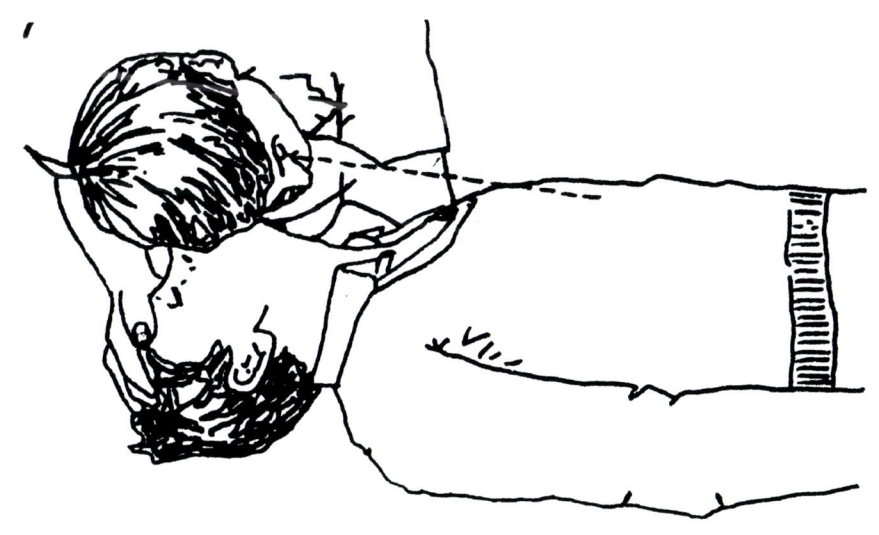

Figure 77 Look and listen

Pinching the nose closed between your finger and thumb, take a full breath then place your mouth over the casualty's mouth. Taking care to make an effective seal, blow into the casualty's mouth until you see the chest rise, do not over inflate the lungs. Remove your mouth and allow the chest to fully fall before repeating the procedure. Replicate at ten breaths per minute until the casualty starts to breathe or professional help arrives.

After giving the initial breaths the victim should be assessed for signs of circulation by looking for any movement, including swallowing or breathing, checking the pulse at the carotid artery (the lower front side of the neck).

Chest Compressions (CC)

If there is no pulse you will have to initiate artificial circulation by means of chest compressions. Chest compressions can only be achieved on a flat firm surface. In a kneeling position at the side of the casualty, find the lower part of the breastbone. Placing the heel of both hands (interlocked) two fingers above this junction puts you at the "sternum". This is the point where pressure is applied when giving the compression. Compressions should be given with your elbows straight, leaning forward until your shoulders are directly over the casualty's chest. The chest should be depressed around 4-5 centimetres (1-2 inches). The recommended rate is approximately 100 chest compressions per minute.

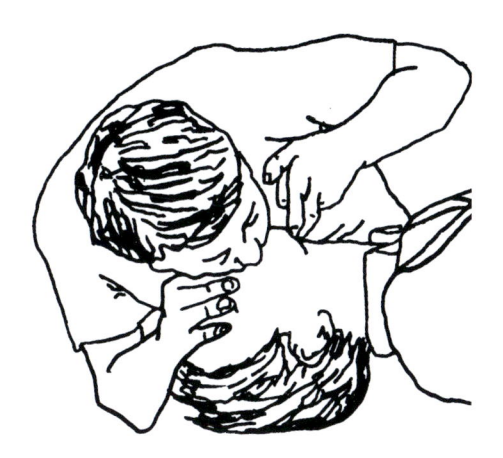

Figure 78 Artificial ventilation

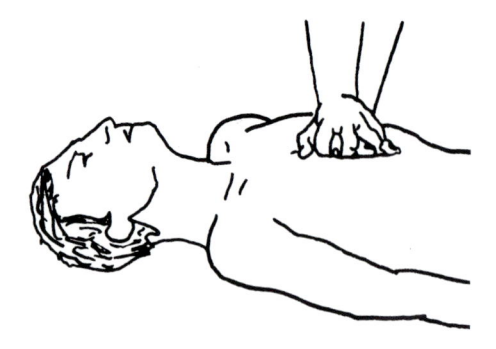

Figure 79 Hands placed correctly over the sternum

Figure 80 Body held straight over the casualty when giving chest compressions

Combining rescue breathing and chest compressions is known as cardiopulmonary resuscitation (CPR). If there is no sign of circulation give 15 chest compressions and continue in cycles of 2 breaths to 15 compressions.

Artificial Ventilation in Water (AV)
This should be given without delay if the casualty is not breathing. Remove the casualty's regulator and mouthpiece. Extending the neck roll the casualty towards you, seal casualty's mouth and give mouth to nose breaths at 2 breaths every 15 seconds. If help is coming to you remain static and give breaths at a ratio of 1 to 6 seconds. It is very physically demanding to carry out AV and tow the casualty. Only tow if it is really necessary. The priority is to keep giving AV.

If the casualty starts to breathe by himself then the rescuer's role is one of aftercare. When on a solid surface, the casualty should be placed in the recovery position. It is important to check the casualty regularly: it is possible for them to relapse, and stop breathing.

Treat for shock
The casualty should be wrapped in something to keep them warm. If they are conscious reassure them. Tell them help is on its way. They should never be left on their own. No fluids or food should be given to anyone who has been given AV/CPR.

Heartstart
At an international symposium in 1990, methods of CPR training were reviewed. A working group was established incorporating members of the British Heart Foundation (BHF) including many of the major first aid training organisations. The result of the review gave rise to the development of "Heartstart UK". Heartstart is an initiative for developing and promoting Emergency Life Support training throughout the United Kingdom.

Emergency Life Support (ELS) is aimed at:
- Dealing with a heart attack casualty
- Dealing with an unconscious person who may not be breathing
- The techniques involved in rescue breathing
- The techniques for cardiopulmonary resuscitation (CPR)
- Dealing with individuals suffering from an obstructed airway or choking
- Dealing with serious and life threatening bleeding

Emergency Life Support Training Course

A typical Heartstart emergency life support course lasts around 2 hours. Course content includes:

- The chain of survival (recognition and access, early CPR, early life support).
- A look at the priorities (ensuring safety of rescuer and victim).
- After dealing with the various scenarios one might be faced with in breathing/non-breathing casualties, the course will move on to looking at techniques in dealing with a heart attack victim, choking and bleeding. Each section will include ample opportunity for simulations.

CPR training is continually under review and divers need to keep up to date with any changes and complete refresher courses at least every three years.

Chapter 9 Diving Air and Deep Diving

Deep diving

A deep dive is considered as any dive deeper than the deepest the individual has dived before. It does not necessarily have to be 50 metres: to a beginner even a dive to 10 metres may seem like a deep dive. Deep diving offers greater adventure and challenge and can serve as an added attraction, although increased care and experience is paramount before embarking on this type of diving. Many deep diving sites lie offshore with the boat journey adding to the sense of exploration.

This type of diving places greater emphasis on the diver's past experience and even those who may have been diving for some years may not be of the sort that suits deep diving. The choice of diving partner is important. The ability of the diver is just as critical as that of the chosen diving buddy. It is important to acclimatise to the greater depths by undertaking a series of dives with progressively deeper depths. It would be unwise to enter into deep diving after a long lay off, or without the necessary work-up dives and efficient back-up facilities. The Association strongly endorses a maximum depth of 50 metres. Diving to this region requires that the diver have a very high degree of competence and experience: this type of diving is not for the nervous or unskilled diver.

Many deep diving sites offer improved underwater visibility, however, the lack of natural light will necessitate the use of a powerful torch. The enhanced pressure at depth and increased effort to breathe will undoubtedly increase air consumption rates.

The threshold at which a gas becomes toxic varies with depth and pressure.

Carbon monoxide poisoning (CO)

Carbon monoxide is a colourless, odourless, and tasteless gas, that is a waste product of a combustion engine such as a petrol/diesel engine being used to drive a compressor. If this is allowed to enter a diver's cylinder whilst it is being filled, the gas will become toxic at depth. Every air compressor should be tested at frequent intervals to ensure that it meets the requirements for breathable air. Garage compressors are unable to supply air to the pressure that diving cylinders require. This air also contains too many contaminants such as oil and water for use in diving circumstances anyway.

Haemoglobin (red cells) combines with oxygen to provide the body with a transport system to feed the body with the oxygen it needs to survive. Carbon monoxide will bind to haemoglobin more readily than oxygen. If this occurs the haemoglobin would be unable to

Figure 81 Diver returning to boat after a deep dive

Figure 82 Divers at 3 metres doing a safety stop

combine with oxygen, which may result in lack of oxygen being transported to the brain/central nervous system and to the tissues.

Cigarette smoke also contains a large amount of carbon monoxide. It can take up to eight hours for carbon monoxide to be totally eliminated from the body. For this reason divers should avoid having a cigarette before a dive. A diver who smokes prior to a dive will be starting the dive with a partial pressure of carbon monoxide that will increase to high levels at depth.

The symptoms of carbon monoxide poisoning are similar to hypoxia (i.e. lack of oxygen).

Symptoms
- Headache
- Dizziness
- Breathlessness
- Confusion
- Nausea
- Staggering motions
- Exhaustion
- Unconsciousness
- Death in severe cases

The only effective treatment is to stop breathing the contaminated air. If carbon monoxide is suspected then the dive must be immediately aborted. Back on the surface 100% oxygen should be administered. This will help to replace the missing oxygen. The casualty should be laid down and kept warm. It can take some time for carbon monoxide to be eliminated, recovery will not be instantaneous. Severe cases should hospitalised for specialist treatment.

If CO poisoning is suspected every effort should be made to inform the compressor operator involved with the filling of the suspect cylinder. This suspicion should also be brought to the attention of all divers who have had their cylinders filled from the same source.

Carbon dioxide poisoning (CO_2)

Carbon dioxide is a by-product of the body's metabolism. Its production can be increased as a result of over-exertion or skip breathing (hyperventilation). Other contributing factors include using full-face mask where there is an excess of dead space, using faulty regulators, or breathing too quickly (beating the lung/demand valve).

Increased levels of carbon dioxide will lead to the body becoming low in oxygen. As carbon dioxide is the gas that gives the desire to breathe, any increase would trigger receptors in the brain to recognise the raised partial pressure of carbon dioxide increasing the breathing mechanism rate.

Symptoms
- A throbbing headache
- Dizziness and confusion
- Exhaustion
- Disorientation

The diver should stop the activity which is causing the situation. Concentrating on a normal breathing pattern will help restore a lower level of carbon dioxide. The dive should be terminated if the problem continues.

Nitrogen narcosis

Nitrogen narcosis, which is better known throughout diving circles as the 'narcs' is a situation in which the diver suffers from an increased level of nitrogen absorption. As soon as the diver is exposed to an increase in the partial pressure of nitrogen, i.e. on descending from the surface, he/she will be affected by nitrogen narcosis. The symptoms vary with depth but at depths greater than 30 metres the diver will tend to be more affected. It is observed that people exposed to high partial pressure (pp) of nitrogen behave as if intoxicated by alcohol. The onset of narcosis is quick, with each diver having different tolerances.

Symptoms
- Over confidence
- Impaired reasoning
- Confusion
- Delayed response to signals
- Euphoria

A diver's judgement and behaviour may become distracted with no acknowledgement of signals. Deeper dives should be done by increasing depths in gradual increments. It is inadvisable to drop down to depths greater than 30 metres without gradually increasing the depth over a series of dives. Even divers accustomed to these depths are recommended to work up dives after a long lay-off such as a winter period.

A diver's susceptibility to nitrogen narcosis can vary from diver to diver. Some divers comment on how they are not affected by any symptoms. It is quite likely that they do not remember suffering from it, or they are not willing to divulge they had been affected. It is possible to develop a tolerance to its effects by repeated exposure to depth, however this should not be relied upon. Any increase in respiration rate will increase the rate of nitrogen absorption and possibly increase the risks of nitrogen narcosis.

The only real treatment is to ascend relieving the pressure. Ascending will allow nitrogen to be eliminated by normal respiration. The dive should be aborted with assistance given by the buddy if necessary.

Some body tissues absorb and release the gas more rapidly than others and thus become saturated sooner. This differing rate of absorption depends on the fat content of the tissue and the blood supply to it. Tissues with a high blood supply and low fat content (e.g. the brain, heart, muscles etc.), will saturate very quickly, whereas those with a high fat content and poor blood flow (e.g. cartilage, tendon, spinal column etc.) will saturate slowly. These two tissue types are termed 'fast' and 'slow' respectively.

Oxygen poisoning

Although the body requires oxygen to survive the gas also becomes toxic at depth. Whilst around 21% of the air we breathe is oxygen, only around 4% is needed to sustain consciousness. The problem of oxygen poisoning is dangerous because its development is almost unnoticeable, and can hit the diver rapidly without warning. Once the casualty exhibits signs of facial twitching it is believed an oxygen-induced convulsion is inevitable. The convulsion is similar to an epileptic seizure.

Oxygen poisoning is classified in two ways: acute (short term) and chronic (long term). Acute oxygen poisoning may occur if the partial pressure of oxygen increases over 1.6 bar. Using normal compressed air the diver would have to exceed 70 metres to reach this level. This is well over the recommended recreational sport diving depth limit of 50 metres.

Chronic oxygen poisoning can affect the diver if a partial pressure of oxygen of 0.5 bar or greater is breathed for long periods (days not hours). A diver undergoing treatment in a recompression chamber will be given oxygen at raised partial pressures increasing the risk of oxygen poisoning, however the measure of oxygen given is strictly monitored with oxygen-free rest breaks given to reduce risk. When using nitrox, the threshold for oxygen poisoning is shallower: this is one of the many reasons that additional training is essential before embarking on this type of diving.

It is important to remember that a diver's tolerance to oxygen poisoning can vary from day to day. Contributing factors include:
- Cold
- Anxiety
- Exhaustion
- Stress
- Fatigue
- Poor fitness
- Hangover.

Gases other than air

With divers pushing the boundaries of diving by extending dive times or diving to deeper depths, they are turning to gas mixes other than air for safety. Use of the following gases is only for those suitably trained in their application. Divers using the following gases follow strict training / diving regimes, which are essential for risk limitation. The first, Nitrox, is available to SAA divers through the national course system. Tri mix divers, who have qualified through a technical agency must register with the SAA to validate their membership and insurance cover.

Nitrox

Nitrox diving began in the pre-World War One era, when it was used to reduce the nitrogen content in experiments. In the late 1970's the advantages of 'Nitrox' diving were recognised by the USA's National Underwater Oceanic and Atmospheric Administration (NOAA), who produced a set of tables and procedures for its use.

Divers have begun to realise the benefits of using nitrox as a substitute for air. Nitrox is simply a gas mix that has a higher content of oxygen. Nitrox is not a deep diving gas and should not be used on deep dives. Divers undertaking deep dives use nitrox for stage stops. At shallower depths the use of nitrox can substantially increase the bottom time a diver can stay without incurring heavy decompression penalties, or reduce the decompression stop times required to safely ascend.

Additional training is necessary for divers wishing to use nitrox with dive profiles and equipment differing slightly from normal air diving techniques.

The SAA approves the use of nitrox for suitably trained divers on club dives at the discretion of the diving officer. Training in the use of nitrox is within the SAA on one of its additional courses. The SAA recognises nitrox training from other nitrox training agencies such as IANTD, TDI CMAS. ANDI and others.

Typically nitrox mixes are referred to as Enriched Air Nitrox (EANx) with the mix containing the following amounts of oxygen/nitrogen:

EANx 28	28% oxygen	72% nitrogen
EANx 32	32% oxygen	68% nitrogen
EANx 36	36% oxygen	64% nitrogen
EANx 40	40% oxygen	60% nitrogen

The SAA recommends keeping the depths to a maximum safe working depth where the partial pressure of oxygen does not exceed 1.4 bar. To ensure the correct percentages of oxygen are not exceeded the gas mix must be checked before use.

The following table represent the maximum recommended depths for the nitrox mix indicated;

EANx 28	40 metres
EANx 32	33 metres
EANx 36	28 metres
EANx 40	25 metres

Higher concentrations of oxygen including EANx 50 are available, however these are primarily for use as a decompression gas when decompressing at the correct stop depth.

Possible advantages of using Nitrox
- Using Nitrox can significantly extend the dive time available without extending the decompression time required at the end of the dive. It is quite possible to double the available dive time using Nitrox
- Using Nitrox can give a greater safety margin against decompression illness
- Divers using enriched air Nitrox have reported lower rates of air consumption
- Decompression illness treatment can be easier if the diver was using Nitrox. This is because the divers tissues will have a lower nitrogen saturation state. The increased oxygen percentage can also help provide tissues starved of oxygen.
- Divers have reported feeling less fatigued after a dive when using Nitrox as opposed to air.
- Nitrox can give large reductions in decompression stop times for a comparative dive profile completed using compressed air.

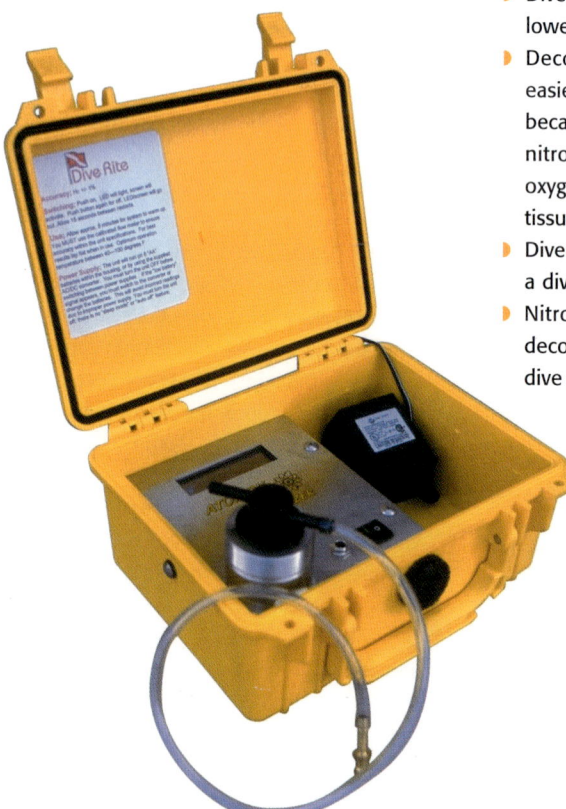

Figure 83 An Oxygen Analyser

Diving with Nitrox does however have disadvantages.
- When using oxygen enriched mixtures there is a greater risk of oxygen toxicity.
- Because of the increased risks of oxygen toxicity, greater dive planning is essential.
- Some dedicated Nitrox equipment is needed including cylinders.
- Oxygen analysers are needed to ensure that the cylinder contains the mix that is required or to make sure it does not exceed the oxygen content for the planned dive depth.
- Decompression illness is still a risk even to nitrox divers. The contributing factors of DCI such as cold, obesity, tired, dehydration etc. still apply.
- Even with the advantages of Nitrox physical limitations exist. Whilst it is possible to dive longer the diver's thermal tolerance may still limit the dive profile. Also the amount of enriched air available and that of their buddy. Nitrox divers using air tables are much less susceptible to DCI than other air divers.

Helium

Helium is a gas lighter than nitrogen. With its effect on decompression profiles the use of custom-made tables is necessary. Helium is not one of the cheaper gases: a 50-litre cylinder can cost up to £100. As helium is not a narcotic gas, within sport diving depths it may be used to replace some or possibly all of the nitrogen to limit the risk of nitrogen narcosis.

When diving below 100 metres the diver usually tries to make a speedy descent to maximise available bottom times: this can lead to neurological problems. Unlike the use of some gases, using helium does not necessitate servicing all equipment to make it safe for helium use, unless the gas mix has an increased oxygen content.

Heliair

Heliair is a gas mix made up from helium and air. Mixing and analysing heliair is relatively simple. A set measurement of helium is pumped into the dive cylinder(s) and it is then topped off with air. As heliair requires divers to complete longer decompression schedules than trimix, it still has many followers because of its simplicity. A big advantage of using heliair is its simplicity for 'topping up' partially used cylinders, making it a good gas for expeditions. Heliair is used as a bottom mix whilst a different gas is used as the 'travel' gas.

Trimix

Unlike heliair, which is made up of air and helium, trimix is mixed using helium, oxygen and compressed air. The biggest benefit of using trimix is that the oxygen partial pressure/narcosis levels can be carefully controlled. The diver simply chooses the acceptable PO_2 (normally 1.4 bar) and then works out the accurate oxygen percentage to have in the cylinder, dependent on the depth of the planned dive. The shallower the planned dive the richer the oxygen content. Helium is used in the mix to reduce the effects of nitrogen narcosis.

Heliox

Heliox is a mix of helium and oxygen more often used by the commercial diving community. Recent developments have seen the use of heliox in rebreathers. No compressed air is used in making heliox. In order to attain the higher working pressures of dive cylinders it is necessary to use a gas booster. Heliox is the most expensive of the mixes with the main gas being used being helium. The cost is the main reason that its use is limited in sport diving. Heliox is becoming increasingly popular with rebreather users because of its conservative use in the recycling process.

The problem of nitrogen narcosis is almost eliminated with no nitrogen in mixing heliox. Heliox is the chosen gas for extended range diving in excess of 120 metres.

Semi-closed circuit rebreathers

No deep diving chapter would be complete without looking at a piece of dive equipment that is becoming widely accepted amongst sport divers. One of the most revolutionary pieces of diving technology to come onto the diving market has actually been around for some time. The rebreather gives the diver an unsuspecting freedom, along with the capability to dive longer and unnoticed, free from tell tale bubbles emitted from divers using normal scuba equipment.

Rebreather operation

Open circuit scuba equipment is wasteful of gas supplies used in respiration. When using a rebreather the carbon dioxide is scrubbed from exhaled gas using a derivative of soda lime. The remaining gases are then recycled. This gas is then supplemented with nitrox from a small cylinder attached to the rebreather.

Using a scuba set for a dive to around 20 metres the diver could expect a bottom time of approximately 40 minutes. In comparison a semi-closed circuit rebreather would offer the diver over 2 hours of bottom time at the equivalent depth. With the method of recycling gas the rebreather reduces air consumption by approximately 95%. This means the rebreather can operate equipped with a small cylinder of around 4 litres.

Figure 84 Divers rebreather

Figure 85 A diver wearing a rebreather

At a depth of 45 metres a diver using a rebreather equipped with a small 4-litre cylinder charged to 200 bar could expect a bottom time of approximately 47 minutes. Rebreathers are neutrally buoyant as well as being lighter than a comparative scuba set. The rebreather is equipped with a buoyancy compensator and breathing regulator all in one handy unit.

As the gas is re-used it has a higher moisture content and is reported to be considerably warmer than the open circuit scuba system. One of the biggest advantages of the rebreather for an underwater photographer is the lack of exhaust bubbles that an open circuit set provides. Without the noise of these bubbles the diver using a rebreather is able to approach marine life that would otherwise be frightened off.

Rebreather training

In order to use a rebreather on club dives it is essential to undertake additional specialised training. During this training you will be instructed in new skills and taught a new way of diving using a rebreather.

Diver limitations

The diver himself is an important consideration when planning for a deep dive. As well as being mentally fit the diver must be physically fit for the dive. With the additional equipment necessary for deep diving greater physical effort will be required and the diver may be more susceptible to exhaustion. At depth the water is colder and the risk of hypothermia is increased. It is widely accepted that cold and dehydration can contribute to DCI. Deep diving reduces the diver's tolerance to nitrogen narcosis with a reduced ability to carry out the dive. The added darkness may induce a feeling of greater stress exacerbrating any of the above conditions.

Mental ability
One of the many causes of diving accidents at depth is through the diver panicking. The diver who is unable to cope with surrounding situations also puts his buddy at risk. The diver must be planning to deep dive and not do so because they feel it is expected of them. Peer pressure is a large factor in divers exceeding dive abilities. Increased breathing rates, less free bottom time, and rescue from depth are all hazards of deep diving. It is not advisable to dive beyond any deep dive plans as the risks are likely to be increased beyond acceptable levels.

Physiological factors
The diver is further away from his natural environment. It is colder, darker and a diver has a higher susceptible panic threshold and any problems can be quickly compounded. Equipment must be in perfect condition and divers should be ready for deep diving.

Chapter 10 SAA Bühlmann Tables, Dive Computers and Avoiding Decompression Illness

SAA Bühlmann Decompression Tables

Decompression tables represent a complex set of mathematical algorithms which are formulated for use in planning dive profiles. It is important to point out that an individual's susceptibility to decompression illness can vary even from day to day.

The use of decompression tables and/or dive computers cannot guarantee a dive completely free from the risks of decompression illness even if dives are kept within decompression limits. Divers are advised to become fully conversant with decompression tables before attempting to use them on open water dives.

The SAA's policy to help prevent decompression illness is to promote a safe diving attitude, which is constantly being developed and improved. The term 'defensive diving' is used to assist the diver and encourage safe diving techniques.

Defensive diving means adopting certain perspectives that incorporate:
- Good training
- Sound training
- A good mental attitude
- Good medical & physical fitness
- Good planning
- Having a contingency plan
- Adhering to the plan
- Diving within the tables
- Safety stop dives only

When the Sub Aqua Association was formed in 1976, British divers were using the RNPL/BSAC decompression tables. Whilst serving divers well, over the years increasing numbers of decompression incidents within the limits of the tables forced the SAA to consider a revision of the tables being used.

The tables became outdated as divers' habits progressed to more than one dive a day, a practice which the RNPL tables were initially designed for back in 1968. The SAA executive and Council set up a working party in 1988 to investigate possible alternative tables. It would take substantial time and resources to validate a completely original set of decompression tables. With this in mind it was decided to review the tables available at the time. The following requirements were sought in attempting to decide which best suited the association:

Simplicity	Tables that are easy to learn and use
Flexibility	A table that gave allowances for safety stop dives, which stay within the maximum allowable times
Multi-dive ability	A system that would permit up to three dives per day (24 hours)
Harmony	A table which incorporated an algorithm programme already used in many personal dive computers

After deliberation the working party recommended adopting the Bühlmann Decompression Tables. It was felt that the tables were the most suitable in terms of the requirements proposed by the working party. The Bühlmann tables were slightly changed to meet the diving practices of British divers and were adopted for use in 1989. A Decompression Handbook was produced, along with a submersible decompression planner. Together with the Bühlmann tables they form the *Sub Aqua Association Bühlmann System of Decompression*.

The SAA Bühlmann Decompression Tables are designed for use only with air and by divers qualified to a minimum grade of SAA Club Diver. During their training divers will dive to the tables under the direction of their instructor.

The SAA Decompression Handbook forms the basis for the SAA/Bühlmann System. The system makes up more than a set of decompression schedules. The format provides a set strategy for managing decompression profiles with diver behaviour guidelines.

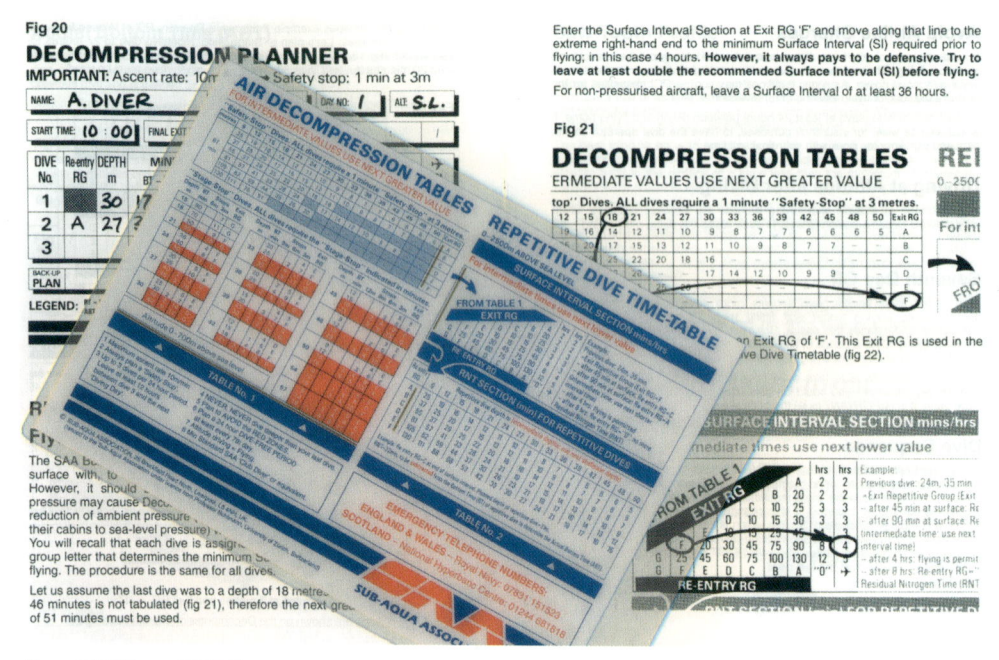

Figure 86 Bühlmann SAA Tables

Whilst the use of other established decompression tables are accepted by the SAA, the association recommends the use of its SAA/Bühlmann system to ensure a uniform standard throughout each club. Each student is advised to have a copy of the Decompression Handbook for use of the decompression tables.

Dive Computers

With the introduction of electronic gauges it has become easier to monitor ascent rates more accurately. They are often equipped with both visual and audible alarms in case ascent rates are exceeded. A gauge that has variable ascent rates may be used as long as it conforms to the Bühlmann algorithm programme. The ascent rate must be one that becomes progressively slower as the depth decreases.

Figure 87 Combination watch/computer

Figure 88 This computer can be detached for protection after diving

Figure 89 Wrist fitting computer

It should be noted that personal dive computers represent the data in the form of mathematical calculations and are not a representation of a diver's personal state. The dive computer is a neutral device in that it would present information to a diver irrespective of their physical fitness levels. The data would be delivered to someone who may be at peak fitness, whilst it would also show the same data to a diver who may be at a higher risk of decompression illness, such as someone who may be a heavy smoker, older, overweight etc. Better models of computer allow the diver to alter settings for diving at altitude or under colder circumstances. Like decompression tables, the dive computer does not give a guarantee of a dive safe from decompression illness.

It is equally important to plan dives as you should do when using decompression tables. Even dive computers can fail. Your dive plan should incorporate a back-up plan just in case of computer failure.

The first personal dive computers were introduced in 1959 by S.O.S. of Italy. Older models of dive computer were based on decompression table algorithms making them a little more restrictive.

The mathematical formulas in modern dive computers are expressed as algorithms developed by Professor Bühlmann. The advantage of today's computers lies in the fact that they continually calculate present depth (pressure) constantly updating the theoretical nitrogen loading of your body. The computer does not see the dive as a traditional square profile and in doing so is able to give allowances for time actually spent at the recorded depth.

Dives with multi-level profiles mean that some of the nitrogen absorbed at the deepest point of the dive is allowed out of solution as time is spent at shallower depths. This means that decompression is taking place during gradual ascents and not set at fixed points. The internal clock of a dive computer continually works out your theoretical loading during any surface interval. This gives precise information for allowing repetitive dives.

As with decompression tables, however, you must still avoid dives that follow high-risk profiles such as:

- Non-limit diving, repetitive dives
- Yo-yo dives (several ascents)
- Saw tooth yo-yo profile dives
- Rapid ascents
- Disregard of decompression stops/missed safety stops
- Physical effort/work
- Diving in cold water
- Deep dives
- Flying after diving
- You must still do the deepest dive first

Modern computers use a liquid crystal display to represent the information to the diver. Internal batteries supply power with some models featuring user replacement batteries. The computer is able to store in its memory past dives, which can be recalled at your leisure or even downloaded on to a home computer using an interface unit.

The information displayed can vary between models but as a rough guide each model will show the following information:

Before the dive
- Function check
- Battery state
- Dive number
- Dive options (profiles available)
- Temperature
- Air in cylinder (air integrated models only)

During the dive
- Current depth
- Maximum depth attained
- Elapsed dive time
- Ascent time, ascent rate and ascent warning
- Decompression stop time and depth
- Water temperature
- Air in cylinder and time remaining at current breathing rate (air integrated models only)

After the dive
- Time since surfacing and elapsed surface interval
- Time to total desaturation (off-gassing)
- No-fly icon and time
- Repetitive dive options (based on theoretical body nitrogen levels)
- Memory of previous dives

Each model should indicate low battery when reached. Dive computers should not be shared between divers as the dive profiles contained within the memory are individual to the diver. On a dive when the divers are wearing different models of computer the computer with the most conservative readings should be followed. Most dive computers use an ascent rate of 10 metres/minute like the SAA/Bühlmann decompression system.

Analysis of DCI incidents

Dive computers follow the relevant profile very accurately and calculate from this the necessary decompression. Tables will normally give a comparably longer decompression rule for the same profile. The reasons for this lie in the numerous calculations made when using the tables. Many divers believe that tables offer better protection against decompression incidents than computers. Statistics do not reveal any significantly higher risk when using the diving computer.

Approximately half of all decompression illness cases reported are recorded as 'lying within the table rules'. It therefore appears that a generally more conservative decompression does not reduce the rate of incidents significantly.

It seems likely that the more conservative decompression with diving tables is still not sufficient to clearly reduce the rate of incidents. In this case, a far longer decompression would be necessary in order to help sensitive divers. This would mean that unrealistically long decompression times would have to be accepted, although these would only make sense for a very small percentage of all divers!

Chapter 11 Open Water Diving, Dive Planning and Underwater Navigation

Open water diving

At last you have completed your theory and practical lessons. The moment you have patiently waited for has finally arrived. Having learnt to dive in the sheltered confines of a warm swimming pool you are invited into open water.

Open water is classed as a body of water not necessarily confined with boundaries. This could be a large lake, a river or the sea. As you still have much to learn your first open water dives are likely to be at a sheltered water site. This ensures your safety as you encounter for the first time open water diving wearing full equipment, in an environment different to that in which you learnt to dive.

You should check equipment as it is gathered, packing it logically into a suitable bag. It is important not to forget vital after-dive items – food, hot drinks, warm clothes, waterproofs, towel, log book/training schedule and some money!

On your first open water dives your practical skills will be repeated to ensure the necessary skills have been consolidated. Out in open water you may experience sharing a body of water with underwater wildlife. Depths will increase; you may even experience a tidal stream and the effects it has on your movements in the water.

The SAA recommends a maximum partial pressure for oxygen exposure when diving of 1.4 bar. This figure will normally determine the Maximum Operating Depth for any Nitrox mixture. However, for the standard mixtures of 32% and 36% oxygen, Maximum Operating Depths of 33 meters and 28 meters respectively are permitted. Failure to observe the Maximum Operating Depth for any gas mixture may have fatal consequences due to the onset of oxygen toxicity. (See Cylinders (Nitrox).

Dive Planning

Dives do not just happen, they must be planned if they are to be carried out safely. Dive planning is important for it to be effective and enjoyable for all those participating.

When planning a dive the following points should be considered:

The choice of dive site
- How many divers are expected/what levels of experience they have
- The method of transport required getting to the dive site
- Expected and actual weather
- The importance of being on time

Choosing the correct diving site is very important: depth, bottom terrain, tidal influences, dive time, anticipated visibility, exit and entry points are all-important considerations in dive planning.

Dive planning should be a shared task with those involved invited to express their views. This is the time to appoint the dive groups (normally pairs of divers) with their respective dive leaders. It is a good idea to establish the responsibilities of the dive marshal, safety officer, and shore cover at this meeting in order to avoid any confusion at the diving location.

The numbers expected must include the right ratio of experienced divers to beginners. The experience levels of the divers can ultimately decide the location of the dive site. If there is likely to be a variety of experience levels it gives the choice of dive site more flexibility. If the intended group consists of quite a few beginners then the site will need to be relatively shallow.

The number of divers who express an interest in the dive would also have some bearing on what site is best chosen, as would the method of transport. It would be of little use picking a very small dive site if you have an excessive amount of divers. It would be stressful if twelve divers were trying to kit up and get in the water at once. It would also mean that there is a likelihood of a lot of divers trying to get out at the same time with the ensuing confusion there would be.

The method of travel to the site can affect the starting

time. The divers that will be towing a boat to a launching facility close to the site need to be aware of the tidal conditions affecting the chosen launch site. Many a trip has been spoilt when it has not been possible to launch the boat because of low water.

The weather can influence the planned trip: inclement weather will make a difference to the boat journey. Even a boat capable of over 12 knots will find it difficult to sustain it for any period of time if the weather picks up. The weather will inevitably contribute to whether it is practical to go in the first place. The wise dive marshal will take account of the suggested weather and also what may possibly be the real likelihood. The British Isles are renowned for irregular weather patterns. There is always the possibility of weather changing quickly, catching divers whilst out at sea.

Many UK offshore dive sites are best dived at slack water (the period between tidal direction changes) so times must allow for travelling to the site and locating the site in plenty of time for divers to get kitted up and be ready for the dive at slack water. The choice of dive site and what experience the divers have will influence the decompression requirements and air requirements. Most divers will plan this between buddy pairs, although the dive marshal must be aware of the divers' planned profile.

Many dive marshals will liaise with the boatman regarding the dive plan. Together they should be able to make up a good working plan, which should be accepted by the divers. Shot lines should be prepared in advance: this can avoid wasting precious time once at the dive site.

If booking a charter boat they will most likely have all the necessary first aid equipment. However, it is worth checking to make sure that the boat is equipped with an oxygen set. An important part of pre-planning is to have a back-up plan.

There are a number of reasons for having an alternative dive site, which may include:
- A change in the weather, which may dictate a change in the plan.
- On arrival at the planned dive site it may not be advisable to dive because of nets, or there may be too many boats already there.
- Inshore there could be too much swell. Offshore it may be just too exposed. Conditions may change en route to the site.

Pre-dive brief

Prior to fitting equipment all divers should go through some of the aspects to the dive that they are likely to encounter. This is known as a pre-dive brief, and should incorporate some if not all of the following topics:
- Nearest location of communication for emergency services.
- Water conditions, depth, expected underwater visibility, tidal information etc.
- Point and method of entry/exit.
- Seabed bottom type and characteristics.
- Maximum duration bottom time with safety stop, depth of dive
- An agreement on the diving signals to be used.
- A reminder of the importance of equalising increasing pressures (ears, mask, suit etc).
- A reminder of buoyancy control and the need to stay with your buddy (regardless of experience/grade).
- The importance of regularly confirming air contents and depth gauges throughout the dive.
- Any skills or tests to be carried out.

Kitting up

The order for kitting up may vary depending on what equipment is being used. However, a standard sequence would be:
- Charge and fit the emergency buoyancy compensator cylinder, if fitted, after first checking the main cylinder is full.
- Attach the buoyancy compensator to the main cylinder.
- Check the cylinder O-ring, then fit the regulator to the cylinder. Connect direct feed to buoyancy compensator.
- Turn the air on slowly, initially facing the contents gauge away from your face.
- Check the cylinder contents.

- Check the operation of the demand valve by taking a couple of breaths from it.
- Turn the air off and verify that there are no leaks in the system. Purge the air from the regulator until needed.
- Put on the diving suit.
- Fit all ancillary equipment.
- Fit the weight belt.
- Turn on air and fit the buoyancy compensator and cylinder.
- Ensure that all straps are free of twists and that the weight belt buckle is easily accessible.
- Fit the mask, gloves and fins just prior to entering the water, ensuring mask is demisted.

Buddy checks

This is an essential aspect of safe diving. It is normally the last opportunity to visually appraise the dive partner's equipment and finalise the conduct of the dive. This final buddy-to-buddy briefing is led by the dive leader or instructor.

A useful acronym used for the final buddy check is ABCDE:

Air	=	DV, contents and pony
Buckles	=	Weightbelt and harness
Cylinder	=	Mini cylinder filled and fitted
Direct feeds	=	Buoyancy compensator and suit inflation and dumps
Equipment	=	Present and functioning correctly

Equipment required can be broken down into:
Protective equipment:
Drysuit and undersuit or wetsuit, boots, gloves, hood, swimsuit
Basic equipment:
Mask, snorkel, and fins
Safety equipment:
Buoyancy compensator, knife, weightbelt, depth gauge, and watch
Breathing equipment:
Cylinder, harness, demand valve
Ancillary equipment:
Marker buoy (SMB), compass, torch etc.

The Descent

Throughout your descent you should aim to equalise your ears early and often – not waiting until you feel the pressure. Descending face to face with your buddy/instructor will give you a chance to alert him if there is something bothering you. If you are descending a shot line make sure you retain a secure grip. Shot lines are there to provide a reference and datum point for both the ascent and descent. They should not be used to pull the diver down to the bottom nor should they be used to pull a diver back up to the surface. Once on the bottom the shot line provides a good reference point and allows you time to adjust your buoyancy prior to arriving at the bottom so you can avoid landing on any fragile marine life.

During the dive

On your first few dives you will have so much to experience. Relax and follow your instructor's lead. Staying close to your instructor will boost your confidence and make sure you do not miss anything. The instructor will use his experience to ensure you have an enjoyable dive. Once you reach the bottom you should adjust straps and equipment so they are comfortable. Each diver exchanges the 'okay' signal before leaving off on the great exploration.

You should be by the side of your instructor, not behind them. Throughout the dive buddy monitoring ensures each diver is aware of the dive time and depth as well as how much air each diver has left. It is important to maintain neutral buoyancy throughout the dive, so that you maintain a position floating above the seabed, avoiding either ascending up into the water column or dropping down onto the seabed where fragile marine life can easily be damaged. This requires fine adjustments to the amount of air in the buoyancy compensator when moving deeper or shallower during the dive.

The Ascent

All too soon it will be time to ascend. This may be at a pre-arranged time, or when the air remaining in the cylinder dictates. You should close up on your instructor. Making the ascent is simply a repeat of skills learnt in the pool. Allow plenty of time to get back to the ascent line with plenty of air to spare. Once back at the line your instructor will check everything is fine before exchanging the 'up' signal. If you are using shot line you should face the instructor and when it is agreed start the ascent. Stay with your instructor throughout the ascent.

It is essential to control the rate of ascent, especially in the final few metres. Buoyancy control is important in order to make a safety stop. The correct rate of ascent is set at 1 metre every six seconds (10 metres/minute). After completing a safety stop of 1 minute at 3 metres you should ascend if it is safe to do so. Check at 2 metres by looking around and listening for any approaching craft. The final surfacing manoeuvre should be made with one hand raised above the head. Just before surfacing make a 360° turn to make sure that there is no approaching craft. If everything is okay signal to your buddy, then the boat/safety cover.

After the Dive

Once the dive is over and the divers have safely exited the water, they should assist each other in the removal of their equipment and get themselves into dry clothing. The dive leader should make a report to the dive marshal, who records the details of the dive. Now is the time for relaxation and non-alcoholic refreshment. A debriefing session should take place, in which the aspects of the dive are discussed. Logbooks and training records should be completed and then signed by the appropriate parties.

Underwater Navigation

Divers will enjoy the dive better if they have some idea where they are. Being aware of where you are on a dive will not only reduce anxiety but in doing so it will reduce confusion. Being in control of the dive will help conserve air as you move about more relaxed. You can assess whether the course you are travelling is away from the point of entry and decide which way you should go should you wish to abort the dive.

There are two methods to underwater navigation, using a magnetic compass and pilotage.

Using a magnetic compass

Using a compass is dependent on various considerations. The underwater visibility may make using the compass a necessity as pilotage may be too limiting. However, if conditions are such that being able to read the compass is difficult, then perhaps you should not really be there in the first place.

Figure 90 Compass fixed to the rear of a console

When using a magnetic compass it is important to take a compass bearing before entering the water. When you arrive at the bottom you should then have some idea of which way you want to swim if you intend returning to a shot line.

After taking a bearing at the bottom of the shot line, you can leave the line in the chosen direction, sticking to the course. To return the divers turn through 180° to retrace their course. It is important to keep the magnetic needle pointing on the bearing you wish to go, with the compass direction of travel line pointing in the direction you are going. This is using the compass in its simplest form, which is a straight-line direction.

If the course over the ground requires changes

in direction then you must be aware of the direction changes, which must be made in the same way. A way of knowing the distance travelled is required when using a compass: this could be using fin strokes or breaths taken. A better way is by using elapsed time, such as a change of direction every five minutes. This is of course dependent on the bottom topography.

Square rectangle courses

The square or rectangle course is one of the easiest courses to follow. At the chosen point all that is required is for you to make a change of 90°. Making four course changes of 90° should bring the diver back to the start position (assuming each leg was for the same distance travelled).

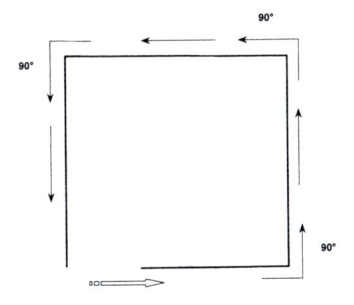

Figure 91 Square compass course

Triangle courses

Although not as common as the square course the triangle is relatively easy to navigate. The triangle course will probably cover a larger area than a straight line or square course. Using the compass each course correction should be done altering the course by 120°, in the same direction, i.e. to right or left.

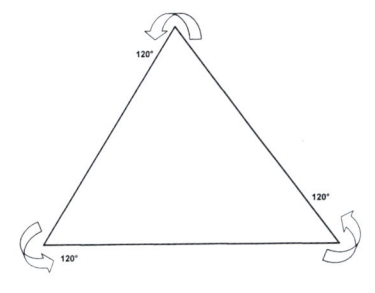

Figure 92 Triangle compass course

The circle course

It is virtually impossible to navigate a circular course without using some form of datum line. It is normal to use the circle course when conducting an underwater circular search pattern.

The most popular type of compass is one that has a bearing window. When choosing a compass the diver should purchase one that is liquid filled: the liquid helps to dampen the erratic movement of the compass needle.

Using the compass the diver points the compass at an object or line of travel; the bearing is seen through a small window. In use all the diver has to do is swim keeping the bearing in line with the direction of travel. It is important to make sure that the compass is held level otherwise the rotating bezel may jam, unknowingly throwing the diver off course.

Using pilotage for navigation

Pilotage is often the preferred method of underwater navigation, and is done using seabed features. A typical example of pilotage is the way a wreck may lie. The divers can follow the edge of wreckage for a given period of time; to return they simply turn around and follow the wreckage back to their start point. The divers can also identify particular pieces of the wreck in sequence as they move along, i.e. from the anchor, past the boiler, along the shaft, then along the mast, then return via the objects they passed in reverse order.

There are a number of other natural features divers can use as pilotage these include:
- Sand ripples form a good method of pilotage. The diver may use the angle of the edge of sand ripples swimming one way on the outward leg of the dive and then swimming the opposite way on the return. Sand ripples generally run parallel to the shore. The diver can make use of the bottom topography in pilotage. If the diver fins against the edge on the outward journey, they simply turn round

and swim the opposite way against the ripples to return to the original starting position, assuming there is little current.
- Shorelines generally slope upwards, any increase in depth will place the diver on an outward course. Swimming in decreasing depths puts the diver on an approximate return course.
- Although not as positive, the direction of the tidal stream may assist pilotage. Kelp will bend with the flow of the tidal stream.

Chapter 12 Diving for Pleasure

Initial dives will most likely be training or exploration dives. But once you have gained some experience you can choose a type of dive that you enjoy best. The following chapter is intended to give an insight into the types of dive that form the basis of this wonderful sport.

Wreck diving

The SAA is committed to conserving our underwater heritage for future generations of divers to enjoy. The SAA achieves this and the safety of divers by promoting sound and responsible practice through its training

Figure 93 Large underwater shipwreck

Figure 94 Diver inspecting a ship's winch

now an important part of our history. It is not just the history of battles and wars, but also of naval architecture and technology that many divers find so interesting. Weather has also played a big part in many of the shipwrecks that litter the coastlines of the British Isles. Rough seas and high winds have driven many ships onto treacherous parts of the coast where they soon became wrecked.

Wrecks can be found at depths to suit any diver, from beginners to those more experienced. There are many different types of wreck lying on the seabed including trawlers, cargo ships, steamships, submarines, liners and aircraft.

Shipwrecks lie in various states of decay and the diver should exercise caution when diving on them. The shipwreck that is in shallow water will most likely be well broken up as a result of the inshore wave action and bad weather. Deep wrecks do not suffer as badly as shallow wrecks do from extreme weather, but will still be in a state of decay due to the effects of corrosion. Steel wrecks rust away, whilst wooden wrecks just decay; they become unstable and start to collapse, putting the diver at an increased risk of getting cut or becoming trapped. Whilst it is possible to enter some of the bigger wrecks, this requires specialist techniques and extra precautions, and should only be undertaken by divers experienced in this type of diving.

Wreck diving requires a high level of experience and additional skill training is available from clubs within the SAA. Preparation and planning is important and should include some basic research and local knowledge.

Divers now understand the damaging effects on coral reefs of poor diving technique. Wrecks also provide a habitat for marine life, which destructive diving or careless anchoring may ruin. Use available fixed shot-lines where possible, otherwise anchoring should be just off the wreck wherever possible. Use safe diving techniques that will not spoil the site for other divers, whatever their interest.

programme. The SAA encourages participation by its members in research and adoption of wrecks for research and monitoring purposes.

Although wrecks are found throughout the world's seas, it is in UK waters that wreck diving is especially popular. Every wreck has a history, and the curious diver will be keen to explore this new underwater experience. Wrecks form artificial habitats, often providing havens for fish and other aquatic life.

Most of the wrecks dived around our coast sank during the First and Second World Wars and are

The seabed holds the remains of many tragedies; the sinking of a vessel is often accompanied by loss of life. Many of the wrecks, which include aircraft, are the last resting-places of those who lost their lives.

There are some war graves where diving is prohibited. A typical example is H.M.S. *Royal Oak*. This mighty 29,000 ton British battleship was lying at anchor in Scapa Flow in the Orkney Islands, when a German U-boat slipped through defences, sinking it with a torpedo. The ship turned over and sank within five minutes, taking with it over 830 officers and men. Each year this wreck is visited by naval divers who replace the 'ensign' as a mark of respect to the tragic loss of life.

War graves should not be entered or interfered with. It may be an offence under the 'Protection of Military Remains Act 1986' and some wrecks require a licence for diving. Wherever possible, diving on war graves should be with the support of the relevant survivors association. Other sunken vessels, such as trawlers or merchant ships, are also the remains of many a peacetime tragedy and should be respected.

Divers sometimes suffer badly in newspapers, being labelled collectively as 'grave robbers' due to those who take souvenirs from wrecks. There are a few divers who see a wreck as an area of conquest, with a remaining porthole as something to take home. Objects removed will deteriorate if they are not properly conserved, and these 'souvenirs' often end up rusting away forgotten in a garage or garden. Taking items from wrecks also means that there is nothing left of interest for other divers to see.

Every wreck already belongs to someone and modern divers 'look but don't touch', but if you do bring anything to the surface, you are required by the Merchant Shipping Act 1995 to report it to the Receiver of Wreck. This enables the true owner to be found. In the majority of cases you are allowed to keep the object (unless

Fingure 95 Diver overshadowed by wreckage in the Red Sea

the find is of historical importance) or you may be entitled to a reward for restoring it to its owner. Divers who actively remove items from wrecks for commercial gain are diving beyond the limits of the SAA.

Wrecks may have toxic material or munitions on board. As well as injuring yourself, think of the danger you are putting your family, friends and others in if you bring hazardous objects ashore. The acquisition or possession of munitions is a criminal offence under the Firearms Act 1968. For your own safety, it is illegal to dive on some wrecks that contain dangerous material.

Some wrecks have been designated 'historic wrecks' because of the heritage they contain. It is illegal to dive on designated historic wrecks that are protected by the Protection of Wrecks Act 1973, unless you have been licensed by the controlling authority. Many of the divers who gain permission to dive these coveted wrecks are awarded permission after attending an archaeology course offered by the Nautical Archaeology Society (available through the SAA). Attendance on an archaeology course ensures that that diver knows the techniques used in diving important wrecks.

Wrecks are not a renewable resource and the SAA promotes consideration for the majority of divers who want to visit and appreciate intact wrecks. Modern standards of behaviour are replacing former unsociable diving activities and only if wrecks are respected will there be anything for future generations of divers to enjoy.

Important archaeological evidence can be destroyed by thoughtlessness. If you think that an object or wreck may be of historical importance, then leave it where it lies, particularly if it appears fragile. Record its position (depth, GPS, etc) and contact the Receiver of Wreck for advice.

Clubs and groups of divers are now adopting particular wrecks for research purposes. Some of these divers take part in detailed structural surveys, whilst others undertake historical research and study the marine life along with changes in the ecology of the wreck. The SAA works closely with the Nautical Archaeology Society in recording wrecks and promotes this positive attitude towards wrecks and the environment.

- Do not enter the confines of any wreckage without appropriate training.
- Research the wreck site before diving on it.
- Leave wrecks intact for other divers to see.
- Know the law – if you must remove an object, you must report it to the Receiver of Wreck. Commercial salvage cannot be undertaken within the SAA.
- Know the law – it is a criminal offence to dive on designated historic wreck sites without a licence or to dive on designated dangerous wreck sites. Respect war graves beneath the sea.
- Take care on wrecks that contain munitions or toxic materials and leave such materials alone. Acquiring or possessing munitions without authorisation is illegal.
- Protect the environment.

This Code of Practice contains the key elements of 'Respect Our Wrecks', a worldwide initiative in which the SAA is a major participant. Look after yourself and the environment, so that wrecks may remain, not only as today's history but also tomorrow's history.

Low visibility diving

At some stage of a diver's career, a diver will inevitably do a dive in low or limited visibility. Indeed for some divers it is a way of life. The dive may have started out in relatively good visibility, and conditions may have deteriorated. Low visibility diving is not to be taken lightly, the risks of separation/entanglement become increased when the visibility is reduced. One of the diver's biggest fears is swimming into a net without realising it. The diver will most likely be fairly anxious and this may have a knock-on effect increasing air consumption. It is ultimately harder to stay orientated when visibility is low. If conditions are too bad or seem to be deteriorating the dive should be aborted.

Fresh water diving

Many divers' first dives are likely to be in a fresh water lake or quarry. These sites offer the instructor controlled conditions where students will be able to dive to relatively shallow depths at the start of their diving career. Fresh water sites include quarries, rivers and lakes. There is often plenty of fresh water life to be seen such as perch and pike. Add to this the normal selection of old cookers, bikes etc, and you get quite a dive.

Inland quarries open to divers make excellent and interesting sites for beginners. The owners go to great lengths to put vans, helicopters, buses, planes etc, in the water for the diver to inspect. These provide a welcome relief from just going in to do training. As fresh water is not as dense as seawater, the diver will require slightly less weight to maintain neutral buoyancy.

Shore diving

Shore diving offers the divers the chance to ease themselves into the sport. Many good shore sites lie just off a beach, with old piers forming a haven for marine life. Sometimes shore diving can mean long walks fully kitted up, from the car park to the water's edge.

Figure 97 Diver preparing to dive on a shore dive

Figure 96 Freshwater dive

Figure 98 This dogfish seems unperturbed by the diver

Reef diving and marine life

The SAA is committed to promoting marine conservation by raising awareness of marine life and its vulnerability, by promoting sound and responsible diving practice through its training programme, by promoting positive action to minimise any negative impacts of diving and diving tourism, and by encouraging participation by its members in research and conservation projects.

Natural reefs both in the UK and abroad are normally inhabited by an abundance of plants and animals, and provide excellent dive sites for those interested in marine life. Reefs come in many styles including rock pinnacles, scars and outcrops, and, in tropical waters, they can be formed over thousands of years by colonies of tiny coral animals. They occur at varying depths, and can be enjoyed by all divers, without the need for specialised training.

Many divers, however, add an extra enjoyment to their diving by learning more about the wildlife they encounter on their dives, whether from the wide range of colourful books and guides or from courses organised by the Marine Conservation Society (MCS), available through the SAA. The SAA works with MCS and is keen to promote participation by its divers in conservation projects. One such project, Seasearch, is a national marine habitat and species recording programme co-ordinated by MCS, and undertaken by volunteer divers who record the type of seabed and the types of plants and animals seen on a dive. The programme enables divers to contribute information at whatever level of detail they can; it is not necessary to be able to identify all the species seen, as even a general description of the seabed type is useful.

Shallow tropical reefs are often covered in many species of corals, and harbour a great variety of fish and other marine life, and offer the diver the chance to dive with prolonged bottom times, not forgetting the added warmth from the sun! Tropical diving is not without its hazards: divers accustomed to diving in temperate waters should be aware of the risk of going deeper than planned due to the good visibility often encountered in the tropics, or running into stage stops if they fail to observe bottom times as they bask in the warmer waters.

Figure 99 A close encounter with a pair of normally shy wolf eels

Figure 100 Many divers favour the shallow reef

It is always important to maintain good buoyancy control, to avoid knocking into, or dragging equipment over the seabed, potentially damaging the marine life. This is particularly critical when diving on fragile habitats such as coral reefs, where hundreds of years of coral growth can be broken off with a single fin stroke. Even touching live corals can damage their delicate tissue, letting in infections that can kill them. It is generally best to avoid touching anything, for the welfare of both the marine life and the diver – there are some fish, coral and other species that are poisonous, and can sting or bite or cause wounds with their sharp edges or spines.

Many dive operators are concerned about the health of their local reefs, and frown upon divers who damage marine life through careless buoyancy control. It is also important not to drop anchors on coral reefs or other fragile habitats where they could damage marine life. Wherever possible it is best to use fixed buoys, or anchor to the side of reefs, or avoid anchoring altogether if feasible.

Marine nature reserves provide valuable refuges for wildlife, thereby allowing species to thrive undisturbed and to restock surrounding areas. These provide excellent sites to observe marine wildlife, adopting the usual 'look but don't touch' policy. Outside reserves, divers who wish to collect animals to eat should take only enough for their own needs, ensuring that shellfish are at least the minimum legal size and are not carrying eggs. It is important to resist the temptation to take live specimens found on dives as souvenirs, and avoid buying souvenirs that are made from marine creatures, such as corals, sponges, shells or turtles. Diving with respect for the marine environment and its inhabitants helps ensure it will remain vibrant and healthy for others to enjoy.

Figure 101 A Nudibranch captured on camera in Devon

Wall/cliff diving

This type of dive is renowned for the scenery it often offers. Many marine organisms choose to live on walls, where the water flowing by provides them with a constant source of food.

Many cliff faces drop off into depths, which are beyond the limits of recreational divers. Complete buoyancy control is therefore essential, and this type of dive should only be undertaken by experienced divers who have mastered the skill.

When diving walls or cliff faces the diver should aim to keep the wall in sight at all times: this will help avoid becoming disorientated. If you intend going deep then all the safety elements of deep diving should be considered and planned for, before entering the water.

Figure 102 Although shallow, the vertical wall is clear to see

Underwater photography
Still photography

As a discipline, underwater photography is possibly one of the most challenging yet rewarding pastimes favoured by divers. It is verification of what was seen on a dive. Telling friends about that large marine creature or wreckage is just not the same as showing a photograph. It is easier to recall memories of dives when there is photographic evidence available.

Figure 103 A housing designed to accommodate a digital camera

There are a number of problems associated with underwater photography. The first is probably the cost of the equipment, which we can do little about. If you are serious about underwater photography then equipment designed specifically for the underwater environment is a good option. Alternatively, normal land cameras can be used in special underwater housings, which can be rather bulky and are usually expensive. Housings are designed to withstand the pressures at depth protecting the camera from the salt-water environment. Such housings are available for digital cameras as well as conventional still cameras.

Possibly the biggest problem for UK underwater photography is the limited visibility we experience. It is important to get as close to the subject as possible to remove the effects of reduced visibility. Visibility can be made worse by disturbing the silt when stopping to compose a shot and so good buoyancy control is essential to prevent this.

Figure 104 Wreck diver with still camera tropical

Many good photographs can be captured in the first 10m of water, where there is plenty of marine life, as well as good natural light. Below

Figure 105 Diver with video camera

this however, the light available is very restricted and colours become absorbed so that everything turns progressively green, blue and ultimately grey. Using artificial lights such as flashguns or strobes can help overcome this problem. However, the light will be reflected back by any suspended particles present in the water if the flash is built into the camera and so a separate strobe is preferable. This is pointed at the subject but is held away from the camera lens axis.

When composing the shot, divers must remember to allow for the effects of refraction by the glass front of the housing, which give similar effects to those experienced with diving masks. Just as objects seen through a mask will be larger and closer than they really are, this is how they are recorded by the camera. In other words, focus on where the subject appears to be, not the true distance.

Photographic shots can generally be divided into two types, close up and wide angle, with each type requiring additional equipment and techniques. Underwater photography is an extremely difficult discipline to master, and requires lots of practice. The underwater photographer can expect to go through many rolls of film in an effort to get that elusive shot. It is important for photographers to take care not to damage the surrounding life while positioning themselves to take their photographs – a single finger carefully placed on a piece of rock or dead coral should be sufficient to steady a competent diver in the water.

Keen photographers are recommended to attend marine life courses to gain a valuable insight into the habits of the creatures they seek to capture on film.

Underwater videography
Another unique way to share your dives with a non-diver is to video it. Underwater housings are available to suit most camcorders including those that use digital technology. It is possible to video the dive and then play back the footage on your home television to the delight of friends and family. The housings like still camera housings can be rather expensive and require careful use and maintenance.

One of the benefits of video is that once the footage is transferred the cassette tape can be re-used many times. Getting good results takes time and practice, however the results can be great. Some divers have video-editing suites for adding titles and text to end up with a professional video of their dives. The end product can be a thrilling video that will amaze friends and family who often wondered why we dive, and what there is to see.

Whether it is a still land camera and housing, a dedicated underwater camera, or video unit, it has probably cost a lot of money and should be looked after carefully. They must be kept out of strong sunlight to avoid damage. Before the dive it is important to carefully clean and lubricate all o-rings. Care should be taken when closing the unit to make sure that the o-ring is not twisted or pushed out of place. Salt and moisture cause the most damage to underwater photography equipment. Therefore, after the dive the whole unit should be rinsed in fresh water and towelled dry before opening any covers.

Nautical Archaeology
An increasing number use their new found skills as a tool, not just to explore our underwater heritage, but to record and preserve it for the future so that we can understand the past. This is the heart of archaeology. Whilst wrecks feature strongly in archaeology there are many other items from our past to discover and explore underwater. Archaeology is not just exploration, it involves properly recording everything where it lies. Nothing is removed until it has been recorded and proper conservation plans have been put into action. All artefacts contain a surprising amount of information, which archaeologists use like pieces of a jigsaw puzzle to build a picture of the past.

About fifty wrecks, out of the many thousands around our coast, are protected wrecks. Some have special historical connections, or are rare, or even unique in other ways and can reveal aspects about our past unobtainable in any other way. Many wrecks are being properly investigated by recreational divers who have archaeological training. It is illegal to dive on such a wreck, except for licensees (who usually have a licence to survey or monitor the site, rather than a licence to excavate) and a list of approved divers. Some sites, designated under the 1973 Act, have a licence for visitors and here divers without archaeological skills can tour the site on a controlled visit. These diver trails are becoming popular and allow divers to come face to face with our maritime past.

Apart from universities, almost all of the training for underwater archaeology in the UK is through the Nautical Archaeology Society (NAS). The NAS Training programme is the most respected of its type throughout the world and is used by a growing number of countries. It was developed from the need to train the many volunteer recreational divers to help with the archaeological work on the *Mary Rose*, Henry VIII's flagship which tragically sank in the Solent in 1545. The structured NAS programme is in four levels and allows divers with no archaeological training to start by attending a one-day course.

The 'Introduction to Underwater and Foreshore Archaeology' is available on a regional basis from the SAA and other diving organisations, as well as directly through the NAS. The course introduces the principles of archaeology, scope of sites, basic dating methods and the diving skill development aspects. The survey aspects of the course consist of the basic principles and techniques of survey, a dry run and a simple practical underwater survey in a swimming pool. This is followed by a drawing up session with a debrief which outlines the common problems and gives practical advice on improving skills.

Figure 106 Pool survey technique practise

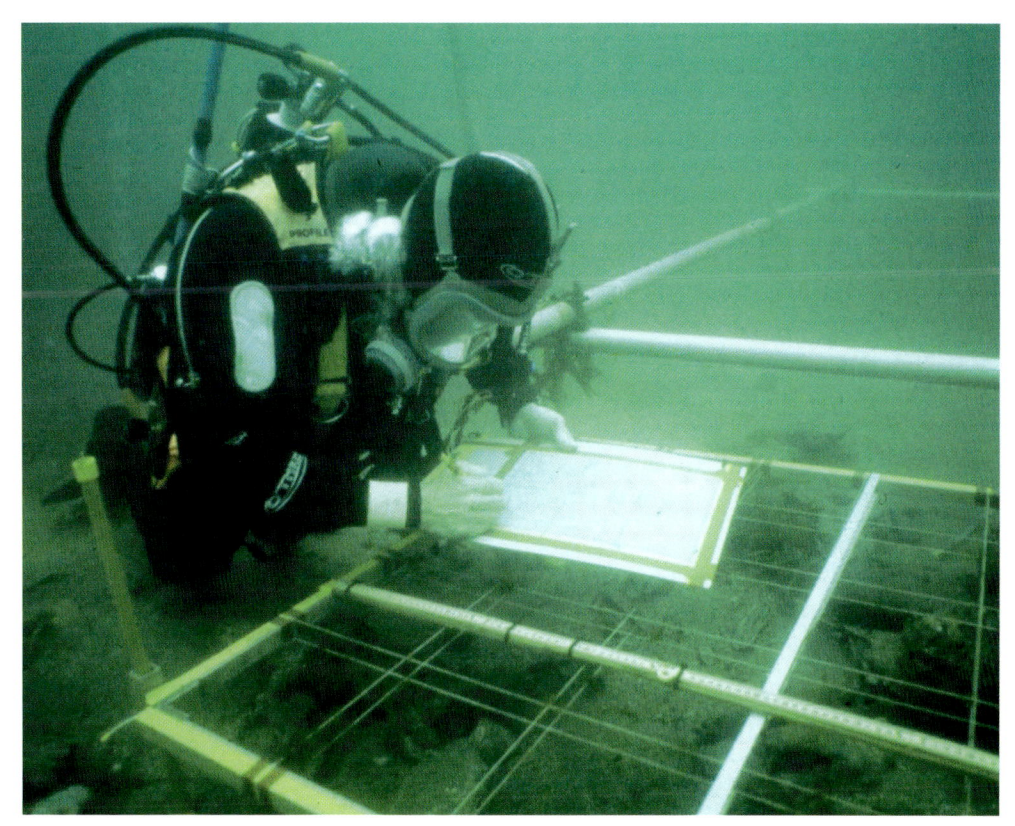

Figure 107 Diver undertaking an archaeology dive

There are also sessions on what to do with finds, and legal aspects. The day closes with an introduction to more advanced courses and to projects.

The contribution that archaeologically trained divers can make to our understanding of our past and our cultural heritage is immense. Many projects, for example the *Mary Rose*, would not have happened without recreational divers and their dedication. More and more divers are realising the value of studying and conserving wrecks and artefacts for future generations to see, understand and appreciate.

More and more divers are realising the value of studying and conserving wrecks and artefacts, for future generations to see, understand and appreciate.

Drift diving

A drift dive is one that is carried out in tidal streams. The diver is dropped into the water at a given point and is allowed to drift with the tidal flow for a period of time, surfacing at a pre-arranged time or point. Normally we aim to dive at slack water and our plans and preparation reflect this. A typical drift dive is done in tidal drift of around 2-3 knots. When drift diving it is essential that adequate boat safety cover is arranged. This means using an experienced boat skipper. When carrying out a drift dive it is essential that divers are equipped with a surface marker buoy (SMB) for diver location.

Night diving

Many people ask why we want to dive at night. What is there to see? The simple answer is that there is often more seen during a night dive! A lot of the marine creatures prefer to remain hidden during daylight hours and will come out more freely during the night. Crabs and lobsters are a typical example, and can be seen sitting on the top of wrecks and rocks throughout the night.

When making a dive during the day the diver often looks around trying to visualise everything at once trying to see as far as the visibility allows, often missing the finer details. During a night dive, the diver's visibility is restricted to what is illuminated by his torch. This means that the diver's vision is focused on a small area, consequently the diver will see things in a far greater detail. This is made more apparent diving a wreck on a night dive that was dived during the same day. The diver may feel that there was more to see, but in reality it was probably there during the daytime dive, they just swam by it.

Many clubs arrange night dives when the right conditions allow. The apprehension of this unique experience soon gives way to excitement for what night diving represents. The site for a night dive should be chosen carefully. Night dives are best conducted on inshore wrecks or in a secluded bay for safety reasons, depth limited for safety to a maximum 15-20 metres. The dive could even be combined with a club social night or barbecue on a beach.

Ice diving/cave diving

Ice diving and cave diving are special types of diving requiring special equipment and diving techniques. Ice/cave diving is not taught as part of a normal certification course within the SAA. Divers who wish to embark upon this type of diving or dives with no clear surface should contact the relevant diving associations for further training guidance. This type of diving is not for the beginner.

Boat diving

Boats offer better diving as they allow access to sites which cannot be reached from the shore. Many wrecks and reefs are more easily reached by boat, with the boat being able to drop divers over the dive site avoiding lengthy swims. Boat dives require more planning as extra considerations are required which include the weather, and launching facilities, sites etc.

Small boats

Inflatables and rigid inflatable boats (RIB) can get to sites quickly, although they can give wet rides. Some of the larger powered boats can reach speeds in excess of 30 knots. It is important that when travelling in inflatables and rigid inflatable boats that divers have their dry suits fully zipped up and wear a suitable lifejacket. There is always the chance that a diver could fall overboard: if the suit zip is open the suit could fill with water with catastrophic consequences. It is important to protect yourself against the effects of wind chill when travelling in an open boat.

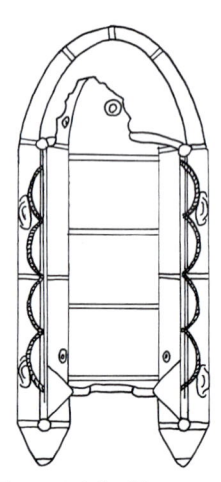

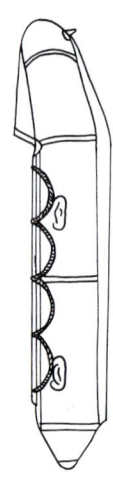

Figure 108 Inflatable

Entry method

As space is limited in a small boat the aqualung set is best set up prior to leaving the shore. It can then be placed securely in the boat for the outward journey. Suited up the boat skipper will let the divers know as they arrive at the dive site. Once the boat has placed a shot line or anchored the divers first in may finish getting ready. The inflatable tube of the boat can be

Figure 109 Divers on a Rigid Inflatable Boat

used to support the aqualung. After doing the buddy check, position yourself on the edge of the tube, make sure that fins are free and the water behind is clear. Keeping legs together tuck all equipment in, then holding your mask and regulator roll backwards.

Figure 110 Diver doing backward roll from a boat

If there is any current running, slide off the tubes sideways holding onto the grab line to stop drifting away. Once you surface, if everything is okay, signal to the boatman, before starting the descent to the bottom.

Exit method

After the dive, with the buoyancy compensator inflated, the divers should pass any small items (cameras, torches etc.) into the boat. Make sure the person inside the boat has a secure hold of your weight belt before releasing it; it can be depressing watching your belt disappear below the water far quicker than you can catch it! Direct feeds can now be disconnected. Whilst still holding the boat the aqualung set should be removed. It is a good idea to keep the regulator in the mouth until you are ready to push it up to the boatman or put your snorkel in. You should also ensure that there is some air in your buoyancy compensator before letting go of it to the assistant in the boat, it is times like this that you realise how expensive diving equipment can be. The diver simply needs to fin up and pull on the hand line to get back into the boat.

All divers should keep their own equipment together and avoid taking up excess room where possible. Space can be very limited on a RIB with a full complement of divers and their equipment. An added benefit of inflatable and rigid inflatable boats is that they can be towed to distant destinations allowing divers more variety and freedom to choose new sites. Most clubs have RIBs because of their versatility. No matter what grades the group consists of, the boathandler/skipper should always have the final say in what goes on in the boat. Although the dive marshal will be in charge of the diving activities, it is the boatman who has ultimate responsibility. If he says he is not happy with the conditions then his decision should be respected. There is always the chance to dive another day.

In order to gain additional experience within the SAA the diver is encouraged to attend one or more of the many courses aimed at boathandling. The courses introduce basic boathandling techniques, and progress through to teaching you chartwork and navigation methods, along with diver coxswain certification. Another course introduces the techniques required for using a marine radio (VHF) preparing you for the test that awards a radio certification.

Large boats

Offshore sites are best dived using a hard-boat. The standard hard-boat for the UK will generally have a cruising speed of around 9 knots, however some boats are equipped with fast turbo diesels and planing hulls giving a faster speed of over 15 knots. Hard-boats can be divided into dayb022`s and liveaboards.

Dayboats are used for getting to dive sites upto 30 miles offshore, and will normally do a day's diving before returning to port. The boat will probably not be equipped with accommodation, although they are usually equipped with a toilet; most will have a basic cooker unit for warm drinks. Few day boats will have enough shelter for passengers should the weather turn bad. The divers aboard a dayboat can relax on the way

Figure 111 Hardboat used for day excursions

out to the site preparing equipment. Only when they get close to the dive site will divers usually get into their suits. This generally means you arrive in a relaxed state not having had to wear a restrictive dive suit for long periods.

Depending on the size of the boat, entry to the water is made by doing a backward roll, or jumping into the water. To get back out of the water the divers normally pass the weightbelt up and then climb up a ladder with the rest of the equipment in place. You may have to climb up a boarding ladder minus fins.

Sites that are well offshore are best dived by using a large liveaboard. The liveaboard generally comes equipped with all the facilities you would expect to find at home including washers, dryers, microwave ovens, and televisions. Many of the boats, situated in tropical waters, are equipped with dark-room editing suites. Accommodation is usually in separate cabins.

Diving from liveaboards is different to any other type of diving: entry to the water is by giant stride; on return the diver will normally then climb onto a platform or up a ladder wearing all of the equipment. Liveaboards can reach sites many miles offshore and often have facilities to allow them to leave port and go out for a week or more at a time diving rarely visited sites.

Figure 112 Giant stride entry

Figure 113 UK Liveaboard

Figure 114 Tropical Liveaboard

An early morning start, a sunny day surrounded by calm waters. A filling breakfast, equipment prepared followed by a long dive on a shallow tropical reef enveloped by a shoal of fish. An afternoon dive, return to the boat, equipment washed and stored followed by a welcome meal. An evening of pleasant entertainment with new-found friends. Sadly time to retire to a clean warm cabin.

A good day had by all

Figure 115 Sunset Liveaboard

APPENDIXES
Appendix 1: Code of Conduct

On the beach, river bank or lakeside
- Seek advice on possible dive sites by contacting the Regional Representative for that area.
- Remember other users and have consideration for them.
- Use litter-bins or take litter home with you.
- Obtain permission before diving in a harbour, estuary or in private water.
- Thank those responsible before you leave.
- Pay harbour dues.
- Try to avoid overcrowding one site, consider other people.
- Park sensibly. Avoid obstructing narrow approach roads. Keep off verges. Pay parking fees and use proper car parks.
- Don't spread yourselves and your equipment since you may upset other people.
- Please keep the peace. Don't operate a compressor within earshot of other people – or late at night.
- Close gates. Be careful about fires. Avoid any damage to land or crops.
- Obey special instructions such as National Trust rules, local bye-laws and regulations about camping and using caravans.
- Remember divers in wet or drysuits are conspicuous and bad behaviour could ban us.

In and on the water
- Do not dive in shipping fairways or in marine traffic-congested areas.
- When out in a boat always keep a look-out for other divers and swimmers and give them plenty of room.
- Mark your dive boats so that your Club can be identified easily. Unmarked boats may become suspect.
- Ask the harbour-master or local officials where to launch your boat – and do as they say. Tell the Coastguard, or a responsible person, where you are going and tell them when you are back.
- Stay away from buoys, pots, and pot markers. Ask local fishermen where not to dive.
- Avoid driving through rafts of seabirds or seal colonies etc.
- Remember ships have not got brakes, so avoid diving in fairways or areas of heavy surface traffic and observe the International Regulations for the Prevention of Collisions at Sea.
- Always fly the diving flag when diving, but not when on the way to, or from, the dive site. Never leave a boat unattended.
- Do not come in to bathing beaches under power. Use any special approach lanes. Do not disturb any seal or bird colonies with your boats. Watch your wash in crowded anchorages.
- Whenever possible, divers should use a surface marker buoy.

On conservation
- Maintain sound diving skills, particularly buoyancy control, to avoid damage to delicate marine life.
- Look but don't touch: take photographs and notes – not specimens.
- Take care not to cause damage to marine life when anchoring.
- Respect marine reserves as refuges for wildlife, thereby allowing species to thrive undisturbed and to restock surrounding areas.
- Never use a speargun.
- Shellfish, such as crabs and lobsters, take several years to grow to maturity; over-collecting in an area soon depletes stocks. Observe local byelaws and restrictions on the collection of animal and plant specimens, and never take animals that are carrying eggs. The SAA recommends that you do not collect shellfish at all, or take only sufficient for your own immediate use.
- Do not collect or buy souvenirs such as sea-fans, corals, starfish or sea urchins – in one moment you can destroy years of growth.
- Ascertain and comply with seasonal access restrictions established to protect seabirds and seals from disturbance. Do not approach seal-breeding or haul-out sites.
- Do not approach dolphins or porpoises in the water.

On wrecks

- Do not dive on a designated protected wreck site. These are indicated on Admiralty Charts and marked by buoys or warning notices on the shore nearby.
- Do not lift anything that appears to be of historical importance.
- If you do discover a wreck, pinpoint the site, do a rough survey and report it to the Nautical Archaeological Society, who will advise you.
- If you do not lift anything from the wreck, it is not necessary to report your discovery to the Receiver of Wreck. If you do lift, you must report even if you, or your Club, owns the wreck.
- If your find is important, you may apply for it to be designated a protected site. Then you can build up a well-qualified team with the right credentials and proceed with a systematic survey or excavation under licence without outside interference.

Don't let divers down – keep to the diver's code

This Diver's Code of Conduct was first introduced by the SAA many years ago, and in its updated form above, it is very relevant to all divers today. However, environmental issues are of greater concern to all water users today than ever before, and so the SAA will continue to develop its environmental presence by the development of the following policies:

- To promote environmental awareness, understanding and enjoyment.
- To promote club participation in environmental schemes and events.
- To highlight current environmental issues, and work with others in order to provide a united approach to deal with these issues.
- To promote positive action to minimise any negative impacts of diving and diving tourism.
- To further promote the Diver's Code of Conduct

APPENDIXES
Appendix 2: Safety at Sea

Even before leaving home, the wise divers should obtain a current forecast. This may save a wasted journey, or allow you to choose a more suitable site.

Before setting out to sea, it is essential to obtain an updated weather forecast. It might look okay from the harbour, but it can be deceiving. The weather may be about to change. Coastguards can be contacted for inshore forecasts in their own area.

Other sources of weather forecasts are available, including Teletext, Ceefax, and the BBC inshore and shipping forecasts on local radio.

Beaufort Wind Scale

Description	Force Wind	Speed
Light Air	1	1 – 3
Light Breeze	2	4 – 6
Gentle Breeze	3	7 – 11
Moderate Breeze	4	12 – 16
Fresh Breeze	5	17 – 21
Strong Breeze	6	22 – 27

Force 4 is seen as the maximum safe conditions for recreational sports diving.

APPENDIXES
Appendix 3: Introducing CMAS

The World Underwater Federation (CMAS) was created in Monaco in 1959, chaired by Sir J-Y. Cousteau, represents all Federations and National Associations and/or Organisations active in the domain of underwater activities and diving related sports.

To date CMAS numbers 162 worldwide members – National Federations and 60 Diving Associations/Organisations pending their status as Federations.

CMAS is a non-governmental organisation recognised by UNESCO (United Nations Educational Scientific and Cultural Organisation), member of UICN (Union Internationale pour la Conservation de la Nature) and WWF (World Wildlife Fund). CMAS is eligible for membership of the IOC (International Olympic Committee), through the discipline of free swimming.

CMAS is also a member of IAWGA (International World Games Association).

It is divided into three Committees: Sport, Technical, and Scientific Committees, each of them supervising the specific activities falling within their domain as carried out by the National Federations.

SPORT COMMITTEE
Includes the following disciplines: Fin Swimming, Orientating, U/W Hockey, U/W Rugby, Spear Fishing, Target Shooting, U/W Photo Hunting (falling within the competence of the Technical Committee).

Fin swimming, like any other discipline, is followed in every continent, with the World and Continental Championships staged on a regular basis.

As regards Spear Fishing, Rules and Regulations for national and international events fully abide by the laws of the concerned Governments.

TECHNICAL COMMITTEE
Its task is to harmonise diving standards and teaching methods, attending to their world-wide implementation. T.C. also sets up certificates equivalencies between National Federation and Diving Schools/Centres. Some 20,000 diving certificates are issued every year.

Safe diving is one of CMAS major goals; its safety standards are currently referenced by all major diving organisations. Federations undertake to implement CMAS safety rules and set up regular controls to keep high-end standards and qualifications for their instructors.

SCIENTIFIC COMMITTEE
It is divided into specific Commissions, with the task of collecting and circulating scientific surveys, notes and articles on biology, geology, archaeology and environmental protection and conservation.

It is also involved in a number of programmes and projects together with worldwide Research Institutes, dealing with sustainable diving projects and promoting environment awareness.

CMAS is the promoter of the world-famous GPIFM (International Marine Environmental Award), in collaboration with UNESCO to honour work providing a major contribution to the conservation of the marine and fresh water environment through the action of divers.

The GPIFM is awarded by an international jury, including some of the best-known personalities in the domain of marine conservation and scientific research.

The above Commissions are backed up by a Legal and Medical Commission.

The sphere of action of the Medical Commission goes from Sport Medicine, with a special interest in pathologies occurring during diving competitions and anti-doping tests, to Hyperbaric Medicine surveying diving and decompression accidents with a view to enhancing diving and training and equipment.

On the whole CMAS can boast 30,000 members - directly or through the Federations. The Sub Aqua Association is the only UK diver training organisation awarding CMAS qualifications.

APPENDIXES
Appendix 4: Marine Conservation and the SAA

Mission Statement
The SAA is committed to promoting marine conservation by raising awareness of marine life and its vulnerability, by promoting sound and responsible diving practice through its training programme, by promoting positive action to minimise any negative impacts of diving and diving tourism, and by encouraging participation by its members in research and conservation projects.

Introduction
The SAA recognises the global importance of the oceans, and that the health of the sea and its wildlife is crucial to the enjoyment of SCUBA diving, whatever the diver's motivation. It therefore encourages its members to help to protect marine wildlife and marine ecosystems by following a few guidelines. These have been put together to try to ensure that divers minimise any negative impact from their activities, but also to promote positive action to improve the condition of the habitat on which our recreation depends.

Guidelines and Code of Conduct
Maintain sound diving skills, particularly buoyancy control, to avoid bumping into and damaging delicate marine wildlife. Take care to prevent equipment from hanging down and knocking or dragging across marine life. If you do need to steady yourself in the water, or push away from something, one finger carefully placed will do far less harm than a pair of flailing fins. If you should need to settle on the seabed, take care to select an area of bare sand or rock. Be aware of your fins, and the amount of turbulence they can produce. Avoid kicking up sand or silt which may smother some sensitive species.

Look, but avoid touching – many marine species are delicate and can easily be damaged. Remember that, despite their hard interior, even touching corals can damage their delicate tissues and let in infections, which can lead to their death. A number of animals can inflict painful stings or bites, so it is also in the diver's interest to avoid contact.

Photographers should be particularly careful not to damage surrounding wildlife while concentrating on composing their shot. Be aware that many creatures are sensitive to light, so try to limit the number of flashes you use on each of your subjects.

Be conscious of where you anchor – prevent your anchor from damaging reefs or other fragile habitats by choosing a suitable patch of bare seabed, within or to the edge of these areas. Alternatively, avoid using an anchor altogether where feasible, and make use of fixed buoys whenever available. Encourage dive operators and authorities to install fixed buoys at popular dive sites to prevent damage from repetitive anchoring.

Resist the temptation to take live specimens on your dives, and avoid buying souvenirs that are made from marine creatures such as corals, sponges, shells or turtles.

Take only enough food for your own needs, and ensure that any shellfish are at least the minimum size and are not carrying eggs. SCUBA divers should not use spearguns. Ensure you comply with any local regulations regarding fishing.

Respect marine reserves, whether voluntary or statutory, as refuges for wildlife, thereby allowing species to thrive undisturbed and restock surrounding areas. It is also important for divers to comply with any local regulations or guidelines in operation in these areas.

When booking a diving holiday, enquire about the dive operator's environmental policy, and whether they support conservation activities and brief their divers on preventing environmental damage.

Be sensitive in your interactions with any marine life to avoid causing stress, and be aware that feeding wild animals can disrupt natural behaviour patterns and can upset the ecological balance between species.

When dolphins or whales, turtles or basking sharks are in the vicinity, avoid driving your boat directly towards them, and avoid any sudden changes of direction or speed. Let them approach you if they wish to. Keep at least 100 metres away from seal resting places and bird nesting areas, or avoid them altogether. Take care to avoid making loud noises, which may disturb birds nesting on cliffs near your dive site.

Avoid leaving behind any litter or pollution. Take it home, or to shore-based facilities for disposal. Be careful not to spill outboard motor oil or petrol into the sea.

Consider adding some extra purpose to your diving by attending marine life identification courses or by participating in recording schemes or research and survey projects, or by enjoying a conservation-oriented holiday in the UK or abroad.

Enthuse about your diving, and the marine wildlife that you see, to encourage a respect for the marine environment amongst the general public.

GLOSSARY

A

Absolute Pressure: atmospheric pressure and water pressure added together.

A-clamp: part of the divers regulator used to attach it to the cylinder.

Actual Bottom Time (ABT): total elapsed time in minutes from leaving the surface until ascent is initiated.

A-Flag: the international flag flown by dive boats to signal they have divers below.

Air: a gas mixture containing 21% oxygen, 78% nitrogen, and 1% other gases (mainly argon); compressed air is used for recreational scuba diving.

Air Compressor: a machine that compresses or pressurises air. For scuba purposes, air is compressed from the atmospheric level (1 bar) to the working pressure of the cylinder, usually between 200-300 bar.

Air Embolism: *see* Cerebral Arterial Gas Embolism

Air Pressure: the force per unit area exerted by the weight of air; at sea level the air pressure is 1 bar. Air pressure decreases with altitude.

Alcohol: mood and attitude altering chemical that is a substance often abused by individuals. It is exceedingly dangerous underwater due to its ability to alter the decision-making processes.

Algorithm: a set of equations incorporated into diving computers in order to compute nitrogen uptake and elimination from changes in depth and elapsed time.

Alternobaric Vertigo: dizziness brought on by the inequality of pressures in the inner ear.

Alveolus: air sac at the terminus of a bronchus where oxygen and carbon dioxide transfer occurs.

Ambient Pressure: the surrounding pressure; on land it comes from the weight of the atmosphere (*see* Air Pressure); at depth it comes from the weight of the water plus the weight of the atmosphere. The pressure at which air is delivered to the diver

Anaemia: any reduction in the oxygen carrying capacity of the red blood cells.

Anoxia: a total lack of oxygen.

Anticoagulants: medications that reduce the clotting ability of the blood particularly dangerous to divers due to barotrauma of air-filled body cavities.

Aqualung: breathing equipment for underwater diving.

Argon: an inert gas that makes up less than one percent of air.

Asthma: a common condition manifested by narrowing of air passages within the lungs (the bronchi).

Ata: atmosphere absolute; 1 ata is the atmospheric pressure at sea level; is measured with a barometer.

Atmosphere: the blanket of air surrounding the earth, from sea level to outer space. Also, a unit of pressure: 'one atmosphere' is pressure of the atmosphere at sea level, i.e. 760 mm Hg. Two atmospheres is twice this pressure, 1520 mm Hg, etc. Abbreviated atm.

Atmospheric Pressure: pressure of the atmosphere at a given altitude or location.

B

BAR: measurement of pressure.

Barometric Pressure: the same as atmospheric pressure.

Barotrauma: any disease or injury due to unequal pressures between a space inside the body and the ambient pressure, or between two spaces within the body; examples include arterial gas embolism, pneumomediastinum, and pneumothorax, eye, middle ear and sinuses and the lung.

Basic Equipment: mask, fins and snorkels used by divers and snorkellers.

Bends: a form of decompression illness caused by dissolved nitrogen leaving the tissues too quickly on ascent; is manifested by pain, usually in the limbs and joints; 'the bends' is sometimes used to signify any manifestation of decompression illness.

Bottom Time: the time between leaving the surface to the beginning of ascent. In multi-level diving, the time between descending below the surface and beginning the safety stop. (Other definitions may apply depending on the specific type of diving).

Boyle's Law: at a fixed temperature and for a fixed mass of gas, pressure times volume is a constant value. As pressure doubles, volume halves.

Breath-Hold Diving: diving without life support apparatus, while holding one's breath.

Bubble: a collection of air or gas surrounded by a permeable membrane through which gases can enter or exit.

Buddy: diving partner.

Buddy Breathing: technique used by two divers when sharing a single regulator.

Buddy Line: piece of line used by divers to maintain contact with each other.

Buoyancy: tendency of object to float or sink when placed in a liquid; objects that float are positively buoyant, those that sink are negatively buoyant and those that stay where placed are neutrally buoyant. Buoyancy control is a very important factor in diving safely.

Buoyancy Compensator: an inflatable vest worn by the diver that can be automatically or orally inflated to help control buoyancy; abbreviated BC.

Buoyancy Control: skill used by divers to remain at a constant level.

C

Carbon Dioxide: CO_2; an odourless, tasteless gas that is a by-product of metabolism; is exhaled by the lungs in exhaled air. Important in the control of respiration.

CO_2 Retention: frequent cause of CO_2 toxicity, usually from skip breathing/breath holding.

Carbon Dioxide Toxicity: problems resulting from build-up of CO_2 in the blood; they may range from headache and shortness of breath, all the way to sudden blackout and possibly death in extreme circumstances

Carbon Monoxide CO: odourless, tasteless, highly poisonous gas given off by incomplete combustion of hydrocarbon fuels.

Carbon Monoxide Toxicity: illness from inhaling excess CO; problems may range from headache to unconsciousness and death.

Cerebral Arterial Gas Embolism: the condition characterised by bubble(s) of air from a ruptured lung segment under pressure; the bubbles enter the pulmonary circulation and travel to the arterial circulation, where they may cause a stroke. (CAGE).

Chokes: a form of decompression sickness caused by enough bubbles entering the lungs to interfere with gas exchange; manifested by shortness of breath and can be fatal.

Clearing Techniques: techniques to equalise the Eustachian tubes while descending and ascending during a dive.

Closed Circuit Scuba: apparatus designed to allow divers to re-breathe exhaled air after removal of CO_2 and addition of supplemental O_2. In contrast to 'open circuit', closed circuit scuba is noiseless and produces no bubbles.

Cold Water Near-Drowning: drowning generally associated with cold water and hypothermia.

Compartment: a theoretical division of the body with an arbitrarily assigned half-time for nitrogen uptake and elimination. In designing decompression tables the body is divided into a finite number of compartments for purposes of making calculations, e.g. five, six or more.

Compass: device used to aid navigation.

Compressor: mechanical device used to compress air.

Compressed Air: gas which is breathed by everyone, (21% oxygen + 79% nitrogen), contained within cylinders.

Computer: *see* Dive Computer

Congenital and Valvular Heart Disease: abnormal passageways between the right (venous) and left (arterial) sides of the heart from birth. Heart valves that are deformed and don't open and shut properly, thereby causing heart failure.

Console: device used to hold diving gauges.

Contents Gauge: used to indicate remaining air in cylinder (also known as a pressure gauge or SPG).

Cross Flow Valve: a valve fitted to the top of dive cylinders.

Cutaneous DCI: skin changes associated with decompression illness.

Cutis Marmorata (*see above*): usually a serious form of DCI causing a mottled appearance of the skin.

Cycling Action: an incorrect finning action.

Cylinder: term used to define the container for the compressed air (sometimes referred to as a 'bottle' or 'tank').

D

Dalton's Law: the total pressure exerted by a mixture of gases is equal to the sum of the pressures that would be exerted by each of the gases if it alone were present and occupied the total volume.

Decompression: any change from one ambient pressure to a lower ambient pressure; always results in a reduction of gas pressures within the body.

Decompression Dive: any dive where the diver is exposed to a higher pressure than when the dive began; the decompression occurs as the diver ascends.

Decompression Stop: on ascent from a dive, a specified time spent at a specific depth, for purposes of nitrogen off-gassing; when not mandatory it is called a safety stop.

Decompression Illness (DCI): a relatively new term to encompass all bubble-related problems arising from decompression, including both decompression sickness and arterial gas embolism.

Decompression Tables: a set of guides used by divers to plan dive decompression requirements.

Demand Valve: the part of the regulator that supplies the air to the diver's mouth (mouthpiece).

Dehydration: a condition where the water content of the body is reduced; caused by immersion, alcohol, medications, excessive loss of fluids from vomiting and diarrhoea or decreased intake of fluids.

Depth: the maximum depth in metres attained during a dive

Depth Gauge: a gauge used to indicate the depth of the diver at any given time.

Diabetes: metabolic condition of decreased or absent insulin production by the pancreas.

Disabled Diving: special diving conditions and groups that offer the diving experience to people who have some kind of disability.

Diuretics: chemicals and medications that cause the kidneys to excrete an increased quantity of fluids.

Dive Computer: a small computer, carried by the diver, that constantly measures water pressure (and hence depth), and time. Based on a pre-programmed algorithm, the computer calculates tissue nitrogen and provides a continuous readout of the dive profile, including: depth, elapsed time of dive, and duration at current depth before obligatory decompression stops become necessary.

Drysuit: diving suit designed to keep the diver dry (excluding head and hands).

E

EAN: enriched air nitrogen; nitrox.

Ear Clearing: technique of equalising pressure inside ears to that of surrounding water pressure.

Echo Sounder: an electronic device fitted to boats to give a picture of the seabed

Entonox: mixture of nitrous oxide and oxygen (50-50). Dangerous to administer to divers.

Epilepsy: condition of the brain associated with seizures, contraindication to diving.

Eustachian Tube: a short tube connecting the back of the throat to the middle ear. Used by divers for equalisation methods.

Exhaust Valve: internal part of the demand valve used to vent off used air.

F

Fin: equipment used by divers for propulsion.

First Stage: part of the regulator that attaches to the cylinder, pressure-reducing valve.

Free Diving: variably defined; in some usage, diving without any scuba or other equipment and synonymous with breath-hold diving; in other usage, diving without any attachment to the surface, and therefore includes scuba diving.

Free Flow: a situation where a regulator supplies air continually to a diver, generally when the valve is at fault.

Frogman: term to define Navy wartime divers and used to describe early sport diver.

G

Gas Embolism: *see* Cerebral arterial gas embolism

Gas Laws: laws that predict how gases will behave with changes in pressure, temperature and volume.

Gauge Pressure: pressure exclusive of atmospheric pressure; when diving, gauge pressure is due solely to the water pressure.

GPS: Global Positioning System: an electronic unit fitted to boats to give an accurate position.

H

Haldanian: related to Haldane's theory that nitrogen is taken up and given off in exponential fashion during a dive, and that there is some safe ratio of pressure change for ascent (originally, 2:1).

Half Time: half the time it takes for a dissolved gas in a tissue (such as nitrogen) to equilibrate to a new pressure, or to reach full saturation at a new pressure. Theoretical tissue half times are used in designing dive tables and algorithms for dive computers.

Harness: otherwise known as a backpack, used to carry the cylinder when not using a buoyancy compensator.

Hazardous Marine Life: living creatures in the marine environment that are dangerous or harmful to the diver.

Hearing Loss: a hazard of diving, usually associated with rupture of round window or inner ear Heliox: mixture of helium and oxygen, used for very deep diving.

Heliox: mixture of helium and oxygen, used for very deep diving.

Helium: second lightest gas; does not cause problems of narcosis seen with nitrogen, and is therefore used for very deep diving.

Henry's Law: the amount of any given gas that will dissolve in a liquid at a given temperature is a function of the partial pressure of the gas in contact with the liquid and the solubility coefficient of the gas in the liquid.

High-Pressure Nervous Syndrome: convulsions or seizure-like activity arising from high gas pressure at depth, especially with helium. Abbreviation is HPNS.

HIV Infection: not necessarily a contra-indication to diving.

Hydrogen: an inert gas, and lightest of all the elements; has been used in experimental diving situations.

Hyperbaric Chamber: airtight chamber that can simulate the ambient pressure at altitude or at depth; is used for treating decompression illness, also referred to as a 'Recompression Chamber'.

Hypercapnia: a higher than normal percentage CO_2 level in the blood. Also hypercarbia.

Hypertension: condition where the blood pressure (gauge) is above 140/90.

Hyperthermia: a body temperature warmer than normal; less common in diving than hypothermia, but can occur from overheating in a wet suit/drysuit.

Hyperventilation: condition where an individual breathes too rapidly and has a lowered CO_2, commonly associated with snorkel divers or divers who may panic.

Hypothermia: a body temperature colder than normal (37°C/98.6°F); severe problems start to manifest when body temperature reaches about 35°C (95°F).

Hypoxemia: lower than normal PO_2 level in the blood; insufficient oxygen in the blood.

Hypoxia: same as hypoxemia; terms are often used interchangeably.

I

IANTD: International Association of Nitrox & Technical Divers.

Immersion Hypothermia: lowering of body temperature by full body immersion in cold water. See hypothermia.

Incident Pit: a phrase, which is used to describe escalating situations.

Inflatable: small boat used for diving trips.

Inner Ear: that portion of the ear in the petrous bone that has to do with hearing organs and balance.

Intermediate Hose: hose between the first stage and the demand valve.

Intermediate Pressure: pressure of air between the first and second stages (10-12 bars above ambient).

L

Latent Hypoxia: a sudden unconsciousness from hypoxia that occurs among some breath hold divers. Often occurs near the surface after a deeper dive. Same as Shallow Water Blackout.

Liveaboard: a dive boat with sleeping and eating accommodations. Commercial liveaboards are usually between 50 and 130 feet long, and can carry anywhere from 10 to 30+ divers for a week or more.

M

Middle Ear: air-containing space of the ear bordered on one side by the tympanic membrane, which is exposed to any change in ambient pressure. Air pressure in the middle ear space can only be equalised through the eustachian tube, which connects the middle ear to the back of the nose.

Middle Ear Barotrauma: damage done to the middle ear due to inability to equalise the pressure differentials as a diver descends and ascends.

Mitral Valve: floppy valve in the heart between the left atrium and ventricle.

Mixed Gas: variously defined; basically, any non-air mixture (e.g. nitrox), although some authors use the term only for mixes that contain a gas in addition to (or in place of) nitrogen (e.g. helium).

Mouthpiece: the part of the demand valve that fits into the diver's mouth.

N

Nasal Congestion: swollen, blood-filled linings of the nose and sinuses, often due to allergies.

NAUI: National Association of Underwater Instructors.

Near Drowning, Cold Water Immersion: see Hypothermia.

Neutral Buoyancy: a state of buoyancy divers strive to achieve throughout a dive.

Nitrogen: inert gas that makes up 78% of air. Nitrogen is inert in that it does not enter into any chemical reaction in the body, but it can cause problems under pressure (see Nitrogen Narcosis, Decompression Illness).

Nitrogen Narcosis: depressed mental state from high nitrogen pressure; usually does not begin to manifest on compressed air until below 30 metres. Symptoms include depressed mental state, anywhere from confusion or drowsiness to coma.

Nitrox: any mixture of nitrogen and oxygen that contains less than the 79% nitrogen as found in ordinary air.

NOAA: National Oceanic and Atmospheric Association.

O

Octopus: an extra demand valve used in out of air situations, also referred to as an alternative air source (AAS)

Open Circuit Scuba: apparatus used in recreational diving; exhaled air is expelled into the water as bubbles; no part is rebreathed by the diver.

Otitis: inflammation or infection of any part of the ear; otitis media involves the middle ear, otitis externa the outer ear (ear canal).

Oxygen O^2: gas vital for all life on this planet; makes up 21% of air by volume.

Oxygen Rebreather: diving set which supplies the diver with oxygen (not compressed air).

Oxygen Set: equipment primarily worn by naval divers.

Oxygen Therapy: administration of any gas, for medical purpose, that contains more than 21% oxygen.

Oxygen Toxicity: damage or injury from inhaling too much oxygen; can arise from either too high an oxygen concentration or oxygen pressure. The first manifestation of oxygen toxicity while diving can be seizures.

P

PADI: Professional Association of Diving Instructors.

Partial Pressure: pressure exerted by a single component of a gas within a gas mixture, or dissolved in a liquid.

Patent Foramen Ovale: opening in the heart between the right and left atria that remains open in about 30% of people, allowing passage of bubbles into the arterial circulation and symptoms of arterial gas embolism.

PDC: Personal Dive Computer *(see Dive Computer)*

Pillar Valve: old style valve fitted to the top of some dive cylinders.

Perfusion: measure of blood supply to a body tissue.

Pneumothorax: abnormal collection of air outside the lining of the lung, between the lung and the chest wall; often a consequence of barotrauma.

Pony Cylinder: small cylinder used for emergencies.

Positive Buoyancy: a state of buoyancy where the diver will have a tendency to float upwards.

Pressure: any force exerted over an area; *see* Atmospheric Pressure, Ambient Pressure.

Psi: pounds per square inch; a common measurement of air pressure.

Pulmonary Barotrauma: rupture of the lung surface from increased pressure of ascent from depth. Usually due to closed glottis, pulmonary blebs or terminal airway disease. Causes Cerebral Arterial Gas Embolism, Pneumothorax, Pneumomediastinum.

Pulmonary Oedema of Diving: fluid accumulation in the lungs secondary to immersion and pressure changes.

Purge Button: button on the demand valve for manually activating the flow of air.

R

Recreational Scuba Diving: diving to prescribed limits, using only compressed air, and never requiring a decompression stop; abbreviated RSD.

Refractive Correction: lens configuration needed to correct a defect in a diver's vision.

Regulator: term used to define the complete demand valve (gauges, hoses etc).

Repetitive Dive: any dive done within a certain time frame after a previous dive.

Residual Nitrogen: nitrogen that remains dissolved in a diver's tissues after surfacing from a dive.

Residual Nitrogen Time: the time it would take to off-gas any extra nitrogen remaining after a dive; in dive tables, RNT is designated by a letter A through Z. Residual nitrogen time is always taken into consideration in determining the safe duration for any repetitive dive.

Reverse Squeeze: pain or discomfort in enclosed space (e.g., sinuses, middle ear, inside facemask) on ascent from a dive.

Rigid Inflatable Boat (RIB): inflatable boat used by divers that has a rigid bottomed hull.

S

Safety Stop: on ascent from a dive, a specified time spent at a specific depth for purposes of nitrogen off-gassing; by definition it is not mandatory for safe ascent from the dive. Compare with Decompression Stop.

Salinity: measure of the amount of discolved salt present in the water.

Saturation: the degree to which a gas is dissolved in the blood or tissues; full saturation occurs when the pressure of gas dissolved in the blood or tissues is the same as the ambient (surrounding) pressure of that gas.

Saturation Diving: diving performed after the body is fully saturated with nitrogen; to become fully saturated the diver must stay underwater for a much longer period than is allowed in recreational scuba diving tables.

SCUBA: self-contained underwater breathing apparatus.

Sea Level: the level of the world's oceans; all oceans are at sea level.

Seasickness: motion sickness or *mal de mer*

Second Stage of Regulator: the regulator that follows in line with the first stage of regulator, and delivers compressed air to the diver, at a reduced pressure 8-10 bar above ambient pressure.

Semi-Drysuit: suit worn by divers for insulation which allows a small amount of water in.

Shallow Water Blackout: a sudden unconsciousness from hypoxia, that occurs amongst some breath hold divers. Often occurs near the surface after a deeper dive, hence 'shallow water' same as Latent Hypoxia.

Single Dive: any dive conducted at least 12 hours after a previous dive.

Sinuses: air spaces within the skull that are in contact with ambient pressure through openings into the back of the nasal passages.

Sinusitis: inflammation or infection of the sinuses in the head.

Skin Diving: another term for breath-hold diving; diving without the use of scuba equipment.

Snorkel: tube used by divers and snorkellers for surface breathing.

Squeeze: pain or discomfort in an enclosed space (sinuses, middle ears, inside a face mask) caused by shrinkage of that space; occurs on descent. *See also* Reverse Squeeze.

Surface Interval: length of time on the surface, usually from surfacing after dive one to leaving the surface for dive two.

Surface-Supplied Compressed Air Diving: diving with the air continuously supplied by a compressor on the surface; can be used for both sport and professional diving. "Hookah".

T

Thermocline: intersection between two layers of water that are of decidedly different temperatures; usually the colder layer is deeper. A diver can easily feel a thermocline.

Tinnitus: ringing sound heard by some divers after barotrauma to the inner ear. Sometimes caused by perilymph fistula and occasionally needs surgical repair.

Tissue: a part of the body characterised by specific characteristics, such as muscle, bone, or cartilage. The term is also used to refer to any part of the body with a specific half time for loading and unloading nitrogen; in this latter context a tissue may be contiguous or non-contiguous, or even a theoretical compartment.

Trimix: mixture of helium, nitrogen and oxygen, used for very deep diving.

Tympanic Membrane: the thin ear drum between the outer ear and the middle ear, visible to the examiner with an otoscope.

V

Vertigo: dizzy, unbalanced feeling often caused by diving problems with the inner ear.

W

Water Pressure: force per unit area exerted by the weight of water; each 33 feet of sea water exerts a pressure equivalent to one atmosphere, or 14.7 Psi; water weighs 1 kg per cm^2 for every 10 metre depth.

Weight: generally lead used to counteract excess buoyancy.

Weightbelt: belt used to carry weights.

Wetsuit: any suit that provides thermal protection in or under water by trapping a layer of water between the diver's skin and the suit; *see also* Drysuit.

INDEX

Note: References to illustrations are indicated in *italics*.

A

accidents 76
  emergency training 76, 77, 77–8, 84-5
  see also first aid
air
  artificial spaces 60
  body spaces *58*, 58–60
  composition 129
  compressed 34, 35
  pressure 55
  pure 34
  see also air supply
air embolism 67, *67*, 69
air supply 31–7
  alternative air sources *52*, 52–4, *53*
  calculations 65–6
  consumption rates 64, 65
  deep diving 86–93
alcohol 77
alternative air sources *52*, 52–4, *53*
aqualungs 14, 31
  techniques 49–54
  see also buoyancy compensators; cylinders; regulators: second stage
archaeology 108, 115–17, *116*, *117*, 124
Archimedes' Principle 56–7
artificial ventilation (AV) *82*, 82–3, *83*
  in water 84
ascents
  buddy breathing 80
  controlled 47–8, 102
  emergency 79–80

B

backward roll 118–19, *119*, 121
bearings 102–3
Beaufort wind scale 125
bends *see* decompression illness (DCI)
bleeding 81–2
boats
  charter vessels 100
  Code of Conduct 123
  dayboats *120*, 120–1
  inflatables *118*, 118–20

liveaboards 121, *121*, 122
planning 99–100
RIBs (rigid inflatable boats) 118–20, *119*
safety 118, 123, 125
training 120
Boyle's Law 56, *56*
breathing process 59, 62–4
breathing rate 64, 65, 69
briefings 100
buddies 48
buddy breathing 53, *53*, 80
buddy checks 101
buoyancy 24, 130
  control 49, *50*, 102
  fresh water 109
  negative 57
  neutral 49
  positive 57
buoyancy compensators *37*, 37–8, 130
  demand valves 53, *54*
  inflation 38
  maintenance 43
  weights 24
buoyant lift 80–1
buoys, marker 41, *41*
burst lung 67–9

C

carbon dioxide (CO_2)
  excess (hypercapnia) 73
  lack of (hypocapnia) 73
  in respiration 62
  toxicity 88
carbon monoxide (CO) 86
  toxicity 86–7
cardiac/chest compressions (CC) 83-4, *84*
cave diving 118
Charles' Law 57
charter vessels 100
choking 81
circulatory system 64–5, *65*
cliff diving 112
club divers 16
CMAS (World Underwater Federation) 17, 126
Code of Conduct 123–4
colds 58, 59
communication *see* signals

compass navigation *102*, 102–3, *103*
compressed air 34, 35
compressors 34, *34*
computers *96*, 96–8, *97*
conservation 110–12, 123, 127–8
contents gauges 38–9
coral reefs 110–11, 123
Cousteau, Jacques-Yves 15
cylinders *31*, 31–5
   capacity 65–6
   emergency 38, 53
   maintenance 42
   markings 32, *32*
   nitrox 35
   pony 53
   regulations 33
   testing 33–4, 38
   twinsets 31, *32*
   valves *34*, 34–5, *35*, 54

D

Dalton's Law 55–6
DCI *see* decompression illness
debriefing 102
decompression 69
decompression diving 70
decompression illness (DCI)
   causes 69–70
   incident analysis 98
   symptoms 70, 71, 78–9
   treatment 71
decompression stops 70
decompression tables 95–6, *96*
deep diving *86*, 86–94
delayed SMBs *41*
demand valves *36*, 36–7
   buoyancy compensators 53, *54*
   clearing 50
   free flowing 51
   recovery 51, *51*
dental barotrauma 60
depth gauges 39
descents 101
distress signals *48*
dive leaders 16
dive marshals 99, 100, 102
dive masters 16

dive supervisors 16
diver bags 26, *26*
diver boxes 27, *27*
diving associations 17
diving (basics)
   ascending 47–8, 79–80, 102
   briefings 100
   buddy checks 101
   debriefing 102
   descending 101
   entry to water *44*, 44–5, 118–19, *119*, 121, *121*
   exit methods 119, 121
   feet first 47
   history *14*, 14–15
   intervals between 69
   kitting up 100–1
   open water 99–104
   planning 65–6, 78, 99–101
   repeat dives 69
   single dive 136
   surface dives 47, *47*
   surfacing drill 47–8
diving clubs 16, 17–19
diving (types)
   boat diving 99–100, *118*, 118–21, *119*, *120*, *121*, *122*, 123, 125
   cave diving 118
   cliff diving 112
   decompression diving 70
   deep diving *86*, 86–94
   drift diving 117
   fresh water diving 109, *109*
   ice diving 118
   low visibility 108–9
   nautical archaeology 115–17, *116*, *117*, 124
   night diving 49, 117–18
   reef diving 110–12, *111*, 123
   shore diving 109, *109*, 123
   tropical diving 110–11, *122*
   underwater navigation 102–4
   wall diving *9*, 112, *112*
   wreck diving *10*, *105*, 105–8, *106*, *107*, 124
drift diving 117
drowning 72–3
drugs 78

drysuits 28
   maintenance 42
   membrane 28, *28*
   neoprene 30, *30*
   suit squeeze 38, 60
   see also semi-drysuits

E

ears 58–9, *59*
   clearing 59
   pressure damage 59
emergency ascents 79–80
emergency life support 82–5
emergency rescue *see* rescue procedures
emergency training 76, 77, 77–8, 84-5
emphysema *68*, 68–9
entonox 71, 132
entry to water 44–5
   backward roll 118–19, *119*, 121
   forward roll 45
   giant stride *44*, 45, 121, *121*
equipment
   basic 20–7, 44–8
   emergency removal 54, *54*
   maintenance 42–3
   sources 18, 20
exhaustion 73–4
explosives 108
eyes, focusing 20

F

fin pivot 49, *50*
fins 21, *22*
   open heel 22, *22*
   pool/shoe fin 22, *22*
   using 46–7, *47*
first aid 81–5
   artificial ventilation (AV) *82*, 82–3, *83*; in water 84
   bleeding 81–2
   chest compressions (CC) 83-84, *84*
   choking 81
   decompression illness (DCI) 71
   emergency life support 82–5
   oxygen 69, 71
   shock 82, 84

training 77, *77*
fitness 18, 77, 93–4
forward roll 45
fresh water diving 109, *109*

G

gases
   adverse effects of 73, 86–9
   composition of air 129
   other than air 35, 71, 89–91
   under pressure 55–7, *57*
   pressure/volume 56, 57
   solubility 57
gauge pressure 55
gauges *39*
   depth 39
   pressure/contents 38–9

H

harnesses 24, 133
   see also buoyancy compensators
health
   alcohol 77
   colds 58, 59
   contraindications for diving 18
   decompression illness (DCI) 69–71, 78–9, 98
   diving disorders 60, 67–75
   effects of pressure 58–60
   fitness 18, 77, 93–4
   gas toxicities 86–9
   HIV infection 133
   medications 78
   physical disabilities 18
   smoking 87
   temperature 60–1, 74–5
   see also first aid
heart 64–5
Heartstart 84-5
heliair 91
heliox 91
helium 91
Henry's Law 57, *57*
history of diving *14*, 14–15
HIV infection 133

hyperbaric chamber (recompression chamber) 71
hypercapnia 73
hyperthermia 75
hyperventilation 73
hypothermia 74–5
hypoxia 71–2, 133

I

IANTD (International Association of Nitrox and Technical Divers) 17
ice diving 118
inflatables *118*, 118–20
insurance 17

K

kitting up 100–1
knives 25, *25*

L

lakes 109, 123
lifejackets 118
   see also buoyancy compensators
light absorption *60*, 61
   see also visibility/vision
liveaboards 121, *121*, *122*
lungs 59, *62*, 63
   burst 67–9
   capacities 63, *64*

M

marine life *9*, *11*, 106, *110*, 110–12, *111*, *112*, 123, 127–8
marker buoys 41, *41*
mask squeeze 60
masks *21*
   choosing 20–1
   clearing 45, 46, *46*
   fitting 20, 21, 45
   maintenance 21
   types 20–1
metabolism 62
mouthpieces 23, *23*

N

'narcs' (nitrogen narcosis) 88
nasal infections 58, 59

nautical archaeology 108, 115–17, *116*, *117*, 124
navigation
   compass *102*, 102–3, *103*
   pilotage 103–4
near-drowning 72
night diving 49, 117–18
nitrogen 63, 69
   narcosis 88
nitrox 89, 90
   benefits 89, 90
   cylinders 35
   disadvantages 91
   training 17, 89

O

octopus 52, *52*
off-gassing 69
open water divers 16
open water diving 99–104
out-of-air situations 51–4, *52*
   signals *48*, *52*
oxygen 62, 64
   analyser *90*
   starvation (hypoxia) 71–2, 133
   toxicity 89
   use in first aid 69, 71

P

panic 76
photography
   darkrooms 121
   still 112–13, *113*, 115
   video *114*, 115
pilotage 103–4
planning dives 65–6, 78, 99–100
pneumothorax 67–8, *68*, 69
pony cylinders 53
pressure 55, 135
   absolute 55
   air 55
   atmospheric 55, 129
   barometric 55
   effects on body 58–60
   gases under 55–7, *57*
   gauge pressure 55

pressure *(continued)*
    gauges 38–9
    partial 55
    water 55
purge button 36–7, 43, 50

Q
qualifications 16, 17
quarries 109

R
rebreathers 9, *92*, 92–3, *93*
    training 17, 93
recompression chamber 71
reef diving 110–12, *111*, 123
reels 41, *41*
regulators *35*, 35–7
    clearing 50
    first stage 35–6, *36*
    free flowing 51
    maintenance 42–3
    recovery 51, *51*
    second stage (demand valve) *36*, 36–7, 51
repeat dives 69
rescue management 78–9
rescue procedures 76
    buddy breathing ascent 80
    buoyant lift 80–1
    diver assistance 79
    diver rescue 80
    emergency ascents 79–80
    emergency training 76, 77, 77–8, 84–85
    towing 76, 79
    see also first aid
respiration 59, 62–4
RIBs (rigid inflatable boats) 118–20, *119*

S
SAA Bühlmann Decompression Tables 95–6, *96*
SAA (Sub Aqua Association) 16–19
safety 11
    distress signals *48*
    at sea 118, 123, 125
safety stops *87*, 102

SCUBA (self-contained underwater breathing apparatus) 15, 31
    techniques 49–54
    see also buoyancy compensators; cylinders; regulators: second stage
semi-drysuits 28, *29*, 42
shipwrecks *see* wreck diving
shock 82, 84
shore diving 109, *109*, 123
signals *48*
    distress *48*
    diver to diver 48–9
    diver to surface/shore 49
    night diving 49
    out of air *48*, 52
single dive 136
sinuses 58, *58*
sites for diving 99, 100
    see also wreck diving
SMBs (surface marker buoys) 41, *41*
smoking 87
snorkelling techniques 45–6
snorkels 23
    clearing 45–6
    types 23, *23*
sound 61
stomach 59–60
stress 76, 79
stride entry *44*, 45, 121, *121*
Sub Aqua Association (SAA) 16–19
suit squeeze 38, 60
surface dives 47, *47*
surface marker buoys (SMBs) 41, *41*
surfacing drill 47–8
swimming 18

T
TDI (Technical Divers International) 17
temperature 60–1, 74–5
tides 99
torches 40, *40*, 43
training *11*, 11–12, *12*, *13*, 19
    aqualung diving techniques 49–54
    boat handling 120
    emergency 76, 77, 77–8, 84–5
    first aid 77, *77*

training *(continued)*
    nautical archaeology 116–17
    nitrox 17, 89
    qualifications 16, 17
    rebreathers 17, 93
    snorkelling 45–6
    using basic equipment 44–8
    water entry methods *44*, 44–5
trimix 91
tropical diving 110–11, *122*
twinsets 31, *32*

U
undersuits 28
underwater navigation 102–4

V
videography *114*, 115
visibility/vision
    corrective lenses 20
    light absorption *60*, 61
    low visibility 108–9
    night diving 118
    photography 113, 115
    underwater magnification 61

W
wall diving *9*, 112, *112*
watches 40, *40*, 96
water pressure 55
weather 100, 125
weightbelts 24, *24*, 54
wetsuits 28, 42
wind scale 125
World Underwater Federation (CMAS) 17, 126
wreck diving *10*, *105*, 105–6, *106*, *107*
    Code of Conduct 108, 124
    diving techniques 106, 108
    licences 108
    ownership 107–8
    research 108
    safety 106, 108
    war graves 106–7
    see also marine life; nautical archaeology

BIBLIOGRAPHY

Diver First Aid (ISBN 0 9532904 0 9) The Sub Aqua Association
The Diving Emergency Handbook (ISBN 0 946020 18 3) Underwater World Publications
Instructor Manual (ISBN 09519337 60) The Sub Aqua Association
Nitrox Diving (ISBN 0 9519337 7 9) The Sub Aqua Association
Scuba Diving (ISBN 1 86126 279 5) The Crowood Press
Oxygen Administration For Divers (ISBN 0 9519337 87) The Sub Aqua Association
Resuscitation For The Citizen (fifth edition) Resuscitation Council (UK)
SAA Bühlmann Decompression Handbook (ISBN 0 9519337 0 1) The Sub Aqua Association